Get to the Point!

Writing
Effectively
in
Technical and Business Environments

Lisa Moretto, Ron Blicq, and Lori Marra

RGI International, Inc.

Rochester, NY, USA
Winnipeg, MB, Canada

Get to the Point!

This edition published 2020
RGI International, Inc.
www.rgilearning.com

This book was previously published by Pearson Education Canada
a division of Pearson Canada, Inc.

ISBN: 978-1-7355062-0-3   (pbk)

PREFACE

When we talk to practitioners — business people, administrators, engineers, architects, geoscientists, biomedical professionals, medical specialists, and so on — they all tell us the same thing; "Show me some techniques that I can use to write more efficiently. Give me something short, that I can dip into when I have to write a difficult letter or comprehensive report."

This is strictly a "how-to" book in which we present proven techniques for writing an informative message or report, or a persuasive proposal. In particular, it will help you when you have to persuade a reader to act on your suggestions or recommendations. Whether you are already working — and writing — or are still in school preparing for a career, this book will provide the techniques to make your communications clear, concise, and effective.

In Chapter 1 we show you how to overcome writer's block by using the Pyramid Method of Writing™. In Chapters 2 through 4, we show you how to develop the Pyramid into a writing plan that organizes your information coherently, regardless of what you have to write. There is a different writing plan for each type of letter, report, and proposal. You will also find numerous examples you can use as models when planning and writing your own documents. In particular, the models demonstrate how the Pyramid Method™ can be applied to every document, whether it's a short email message, a one-page letter or memorandum, a five-page report, or a fifty-page proposal.

Chapter 5 shows you how to design a document to increase its readability and direct a reader's attention to key information. It also introduces you to techniques for writing to readers in other cultures—an essential skill in our increasingly global marketplace.

Chapter 6 suggests way to sharpen the words you use and the sentences you write so they are direct and definite, neither too abrupt nor too wordy, and give your readers confidence in you as an effective conveyor of information. It also includes exercises so you can test the skills you have learned.

We suggest that before you go straight to the chapter and section that gives you the advice you need, you first read Chapters 1 and 2. They will introduce you to the Pyramid Method of Writing ™ and show you how to apply it. That method forms the foundation for this book's advice.

ABOUT THE AUTHORS

Ron Blicq is a founding member of RGI International. He has extensive experience as a technical writer and editor with the Royal Air Force in Britain and CAE Industries Limited in Canada, and has been teaching technical and business communications since 1967. He is a Fellow of both the Society for Technical Communication and the Association of Teachers of Technical Writing and is a Life Member of the Institute of Electrical and Electronics Engineers Inc. (IEEE). Ron lives in Winnipeg, Manitoba.

Lisa Moretto is President of RGI International. She has taught technical communication and leadership development to engineers and technical professionals for over 25 years. She has been an Information Developer for IBM and a Learning Products Engineer for Hewlett-Packard in the U.K. Lisa holds a B.Sc. in Technical Communication from Clarkson University and an M.Sc. in User Interface Design from London Guildhall University. She is a member of both the Society for Technical Communication and the Institute of Electrical and Electronics Engineers Inc. (IEEE).

Lori Marra is Vice President of RGI International. She completed a thirty-year career in technical communication and leadership development, working for several international companies including Johnson & Johnson, Kodak, and Carestream. In 2015, Lori launched RGI International's Center for Technical and Engineering Leadership (CTEL). She is a full-time professor at the Rochester Institute of Technology where she teaches Technical Communication. Lori is an Associate Fellow of the Society for Technical Communication.

Chapter 1

GETTING STARTED

If you are like most people, you find it difficult to start a writing project. It doesn't matter if it's a short email to your staff, a complaint letter, or a formal proposal. You stare at the computer screen or the blank page and wait for inspiration. Or you pour a cup of coffee or stroll around the office, but neither seems to bring inspiration. You know you are wasting your time *and* the company's money. It's frustrating.

When you do finally settle down and start writing, you may find that your words come easily and seem to flow. Sometimes though, the words flow too easily and you may end up rambling. This is what we call a "brain dump," and the result is often a very confusing, unorganized piece of writing that's very difficult for your audience to read. You've probably received information written like this. As you read it, you keep wondering when the writer is going to get to the point. And if you happened to read the whole message, you still may not be sure what is expected of you.

This is just one of many common problems writers have. You're not alone. We're going to introduce you to some techniques we've been teaching people for over 40 years—tried and true and very effective in the technical and business worlds. They will help you become a quicker, more effective and efficient writer by showing you how to

- identify your audience,

- identify the primary information for that audience,

- focus the reader's attention on the primary information,

- easily get started,

- understand the difference between a tell and a sell message, and

- learn to structure your writing.

Identifying the Audience

Before you sit down to write *anything*, you need to know who you are writing to and what they need to know from you. This is one of the most common problems people have when they try to communicate information — they haven't properly identified their audience.

You need to ask yourself some questions about your reader. Often you will know exactly who you are writing to, in which case it is relatively easy to identify what information that particular person (or people) wants or needs from you. In some cases, you may have communicated with the person before. However, there will be other times when you will not personally know your reader, and on these occasions, you have to identify the *types* of person (or people) who will be reading your writing. This may occur if, for example, you are writing operating instructions for a new software program or responding to a request for a proposal for a government contract.

Ask Questions

When you have a reader in mind, ask yourself five specific questions about that person:

1. What does my reader want to know?
2. What does my reader need to be told?
3. What does my reader already know about this subject?
4. Who else is likely to read my correspondence?
5. If there is more than one reader, who will make a decision based on the information I am developing?

1. **What does my reader want to know?**

Every audience has a reason or purpose for choosing to read your writing. You must focus on what their reason is, not what you feel you want to tell him or her.

2. **What does my reader need to be told?**

There may be a significant difference between what a reader would like to hear and what a reader needs to hear (as in the case of a client who expects you to report that a job is complete, and who has to be told that it is not).

3. **What does my reader already know about this subject?**

Understanding what he or she knows about the subject will help you identify where to start and how much background information to include.

4. **Who else is likely to read my letter or report?**

There may be secondary readers to whom the document will be circulated and you need to identify their knowledge level and interests, too.

5. **If there is more than one reader, who will make a decision based on the information I'm writing?**

The person making the decision(s) will be your primary reader. This will also be the person to whom you direct the key information.

Identifying your audience will not only help you direct your message but it will also help you choose the most appropriate tone and language.

Focus the Message

Once you identify who you are writing to and what they most need to know from you, you have to position that information so it gets the attention it deserves. At school, we were taught to use the "climactic" method of writing that encouraged us to write all our facts down first, before we could make our main point. This allowed the reader to understand all the events or circumstances that led up to the main message. Usually the points were listed chronologically.

As adults, we are still influenced by our education and often still write in the climactic style. Unfortunately, this method isn't appropriate for business and technical communication. Let's look at an example. In Figure 1-1, it's apparent that Alan Cairn, Vancourt Business Systems' chief purchasing agent uses the climactic method of writing to describe an order mix-up in an email sent to senior accountant Pranet Vishu.

Dear Pranet:

On September 5, I ordered a case of spindles from Cardorinth Importers for $267.80. The purchase order number was 41258. When, a week later, the Assembly Department said their need was urgent, I phoned Cardorinth and asked them to expedite the order. As a precaution, I followed up with an email message on September 13 asking them to send it to me overnight.

Unfortunately, my email quoted an erroneous PO number (41528 instead of 41258), which Cardorinth treated as a second order. This second order arrived first, on September 19, and was accepted by the Material Control Department as belonging to PO 41258 without the discrepancy in purchase order numbers being noticed.

Then, when the original order eventually arrived on September 26, it also was accepted by Material Control. The Assembly Department has since used parts from both shipments, so we cannot return either of them.

Because we have used PO number 41528 for another order to a different supplier, I have authorized Cardorinth Importers to invoice us for both cases of spindles against PO number 41258. So please change the quantity for "two cases" and the amount to "$535.60" on your copy of the purchase order, and pay Cardorinth $535.60 against their invoice No. 2253.

Figure 1-1:   An email using the climactic method

Although Pranet will understand what the situation is and what Alan is trying to tell him, he has to read the entire message before he learns that something is expected of him. In today's hectic business environment, we are often interrupted by text messages, phone calls, meetings, or someone needing our attention. We, who initiate the message, must make it easy and quick for our audience to determine the main point of our communication. In our example, Alan has taken the risk that Pranet may be interrupted and may not read to the end of his message. He may never understand that he has to take an action. Alan would have been better off if he had identified the main message for Pranet — the most important information — and placed it right up front. That way, Pranet would immediately know his reason for writing. We call this "the immediate" method of writing. Figure 1-2 graphically compares the climactic and immediate methods of writing. Notice the amount of time it takes for the reader to get to the main message in each. Also notice that all of the information is conveyed in both messages. However in the immediate method, the main message is right at the beginning, where the audience needs it most.

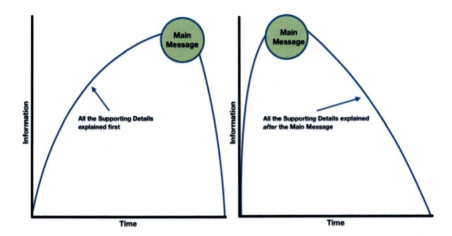

Figure 1-2:   A graphical comparison of climactic vs immediate method of conveying information

To use the immediate method, Alan must first identify his audience, which means asking himself these questions:

1. Who is my reader?

Pranet Vishu, Senior Accountant

2. What does my reader need to be told?

That there is a problem with the purchase order quantities.

3. What does he already know about this subject?

Very little, except that he has a copy of the original purchase order (No. 41258)

4. Who else is likely to read my email?

No one in this situation.

5. What does he most want or need to know?

He has to alter his copy of PO 41258 by changing the quantity ordered and the total dollar figure.

With the information gained from this quick audience analysis, Alan is ready to rewrite his email to Pranet. This time he puts the main message in the first paragraph:

To correct an ordering error, please change the quantity only and total amount entries on PO 41258 from "1"to "2," and "$267.80" to "$535.60." This will make our purchase order agree with Cardorinth Importers, invoice No. 2253.

Figure 1-3:   Rewriting the main message

If you place this main message at the beginning of Alan's original email, you will notice the email makes much more sense. When you know Alan's *reason* for writing, you don't have to keep wondering, "Why am I reading this?" Pranet will now exactly what's expected of him after reading the first paragraph. Also, with the main information right up front, Alan can edit out many of the details he previously included, which will result in a much shorter, concise email. Wouldn't we all like shorter, more concise emails these days?

Divide the Information

Once you decide what the main message is, you then need to decide what details are necessary to support that message. In Alan's case he needs to ask himself: "If I was Pranet, what else would I want to now after reading the main message?", to which he might reply:

1.   What caused the error?
2.   Why do the changes need to be made and what effect will they have?

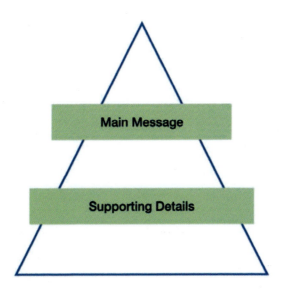

Figure 1-4: The basic Pyramid structure

The answers to these questions become the supporting details and are placed immediately following the main message. You can visualize this information in two distinct blocks: The main message (from now on we refer to it as the Summary Statement) is what the reader most needs to know. The Supporting Details answers any questions the reader may have after reading the Summary Statement: *What? Who? When? Where? Why? How?* Figure 1-4 illustrates this concept.

In Figure 1-5, Alan's memo to Pranet has been rewritten using the immediate method. The first paragraph contains the Summary Statement and the remaining paragraphs give the Supporting Details. Using these compartments as building blocks helps you construct clear, concise, and effective email, letters, reports, and really any type of message. In later chapters, we will explain the compartments and adapt them to various situations you will encounter in technical and business communications.

Summary Statement

Supporting Details

Dear Pranet:

To correct an ordering error, please change the quantity only and total amount entries on PO 41258 from "1"to "2," and "$267.80" to "$535.60." This will make our purchase order agree with Cardorinth Importers, invoice No. 2253.

The error occurred when we inadvertently referred to PO 41528 (instead of 41258) in an email message to Cardorinth, which they interpreted as an additional order for spindles. The error was compounded twice: first by Material Control, which accepted both shipments against PO 41258, and then by Assembly, which opened and used parts from both shipments.

To avoid further complications (and because we have used PO number 41528 to purchase goods from a different supplier), I have authorized Cardorinth Importers to transfer the order for spindles they supplied against PO 41528 onto PO 41258, and to invoice us for both shipments on the one order.

Sincerely,

Alan

Figure 1-5: Using writing compartments to structure a message

Finding the Words to Start

Most people prefer to read letters that have the main message right up front because they are easier to understand and simplify their work. Some writers, however, have difficulty finding the right words to formulate their opening sentences. After all, we were taught to write using the climactic method, and we've been writing that way most if not all of our lives. To overcome this difficulty, imagine your reader is right in front of you and has asked: "What do you *most* want to tell me?" When you answer that question you will have identified your main message or Summary Statement.

To help you find the right words we suggest that, before you start writing, you first jot down these six words,

I want to tell you that...

and then finish the sentence.

For example,

I want to tell you that, starting November 8, all staff must register their software with the Information Technology (IT) Department.

Once you finish writing the sentence, delete the six introductory words. We call them the six "hidden words" because they are not needed to convey the message. They just help focus you on putting your main message at the beginning of your communication

Starting November 8, all staff must register their software with the Information Technology (IT) Department.

If you use this technique each time you write a message, it will help you start writing quickly; it will also ensure the main message is at the beginning. Below are more examples of opening sentences.

I want to tell you that...

- Our purchase order No. W1143 has been cancelled.

- Louise McKenzie will be representing Floral West Imports Ltd. at the Western Purchasing Agent's meeting on November 6.

- We have experienced ten breakdowns with the BX-7 box stapler we purchased from you and request that you replace it with a more reliable model.

- Your order was shipped air express on May 15 and you should have received it the following morning.

- Our customs brokers have received only three of the four cartons listed on invoice C2827 and will not clear the shipment until they receive the fourth carton.

Sometimes your Summary Statement may seem too abrupt or impolite when the six hidden words are removed. For example, in a situation like this, you need some additional words to soften the unwanted message so it isn't so abrupt.

Dear Ms. Darwin:

Your June 10 order for 80 video boards cannot be filled until mid-October.

Dear Ms. Darwin:

I regret that your June 10 order for 80 video boards cannot be filled until mid-October.

If you phrase your Summary Statement as a question or a direct instruction, the six hidden words won't work. However, using these techniques is another way to force the main message into the first paragraph. For example,

May I have your approval to attend a one-week management training course at the University of Manitoba from March 10-14?

Can you install a staircase between area K7 and our administration area immediately above it?

Please cancel our purchase order W1143, dated May 5.

Avoid False Starts

A false start uses wasteful, unnecessary words that make it seem like you are "spinning your wheels" or really going nowhere with your message. We see so many other people use them in their writing that we tend, almost automatically, to insert them as the openings to our letters and emails. We call these false starts because they draw you into a long, convoluted sentence that is difficult to understand and difficult to punctuate properly. These false starts can also take you off course from your main message. For example,

Dear Mr. Kosty:

With reference to your letter of November 19, in which you describe the discoloration of our paint color No. 188 when used as a second coat on top of primer No. 145, we have conducted an investigation into your problems. Our conclusion is that the paint you used may have exceeded its shelf life.

Notice how *"I want to tell you that…"* doesn't work with this opening sentence. You cannot place it at the beginning and create a coherent sentence. If the opening was started like this, it would be more focused and concise:

Dear Mr. Kosty:

We have investigated the problem of paint discoloration described in your November 19 letter, and have concluded that the paint you used may have exceeded its self-life.

Now you can place *"I want to tell you that…"* at the beginning of the sentence and it makes sense.

An Unimaginative, Directionless Start

Here are more examples of false starts and some warnings!
Never start with a word that ends in "-ing":

Referring…
Replying…

Never start with an expression that ends with the preposition "to":

With reference to…
In answer to…
Pursuant to…
Due to…

The "-ing" words and "to" phrases may cause you to ramble and punctuate incorrectly. The "to" phrase in the first letter to Mr. Kosty created a rambling introductory sentence that told Mr. Kosty all about what he had already written! That's not the main message.

Never start with a redundant expression:

I am writing…
For your information…
This is to inform you…
The purpose of this letter is…
We have received your letter…

A reader can *see* that you are writing, *knows* you are writing to impart information, and *is aware* that you wouldn't be replying if you *hadn't* received his or her letter. You can take all of these expressions out and not change the meaning in your message.

Never send the reader on a hunt:

Enclosed please find…
Why? Did you lose it?

Attached herewith
Wow, that's old fashioned and legal-talk. If you say something is *attached*, it's redundant to also say it's *here*.

Try writing simply:
Here is…
Attached is…

A Strong, Focused Start

Always remember the "six hidden words":

> **I want to tell you that…**

If you consistently open each email or letter with these words (and later delete them), you will never again make a false start. Whenever you write an email or letter, test the opening sentence by inserting the six hidden words to see if the opening makes sense.

Identifying Your Purpose for Writing

We've already discussed the importance of identifying your audience or reader, but before you start writing, you also need to answer one more question: "What is the purpose of this communication?" People often answer in vague statements like:

- I have to report on the progress of our index-conversion program.

- I want more storage space, so I'm asking for additional cloud space.

- I have to explain how we conducted our robotics research.

- I need approval to send two of my staff to a proposal-writing seminar.

These responses show the writers are more concerned with their own needs than with their reader's needs. The writers have not identified *what they want their readers to do or what their readers need to know*.

Before you begin typing at a keyboard, decide what kind of message you want to convey. This is true for *any* communication, emails, text messages, letters, reports, or proposals. There are only two kinds of messages to choose from:

- Messages that *tell* about facts and events. (Informative writing)
- Messages that *sell* an idea or concept. (Persuasive writing)

Tell Messages

Communications that *tell* are primarily *informative*; they simply pass along information and do not expect the reader to respond. So, these communications need to be clear, concise, and definite. Because tell messages refer to tangibles (facts, events, occurrences, and happenings), you can get straight to the point and describe only the essential details. A tell message can also be an instruction that directs somebody to do something. After reading a tell message the reader's reaction is simply to say or mentally comment, "OK, that's interesting. Now I know."

Sell Messages

Communications that *sell* have to be *persuasive*: they present an idea or concept and require the reader to act or react, by agreeing with, approving, or implementing the idea, suggestion, or proposal. So, if your reader is to react in the way you want, your communication must be *convincing*.

Because sell messages refer to intangibles (ideas, concepts, suggestions, and proposals), you must develop the background and details in sufficient depth to ensure that the reader has all the information he or she needs to make a decision or to take the appropriate action. You should, though, avoid presenting too much information, which might make your message obscure. First you need to decide your purpose for writing and the response you want from your reader. Ask yourself:

- Am I *requesting* something?
- Am I *proposing* that something be done?
- Do I want *approval* to do something?

After reading a sell message, the reader's reaction might be something like, "You have a good point! I'll get right to it." If you have written an effective opening with the main message right up front, the reader of a sell message *knows exactly what response is expected.*

Examples of Tell and Sell Messages

Here are two messages: one is a tell and one is a sell. In both situations Richard is writing to his manager.

Tell Message

Dear Susan:

The RMF project is three days behind schedule, but we will make up the time and be back on schedule by March 1. We will be able to deliver the project to the client on the planned April 13 date.

We have two engineers absent because of an illness for two weeks and an equipment failure set us back two days. The JCT group was able to lend us one of their computers while ours was being repaired. Each member of the team is able to work three hours overtime each week for the next two weeks, which will ensure that we are back on schedule by March 1.

Sincerely,

Richard

Richard does not expect a response from Susan. The purpose of this message is to simply inform her of the delay and to explain what will be done to get the project back on schedule.

Sell Message

Dear Susan:

The RMF project is three days behind schedule and unless we receive your approval to transfer one engineer and one computer to us, we will not be able to deliver the project to the client on April 13, as promised.

We had two engineers absent because of illness for two weeks and an equipment failure set us back two days. To make up this lost time we need an engineer and a computer transferred from the JCT project to the RMF project for three weeks.

Please let me know by February 15 if you approve this request so I can begin working on the transfer and reschedule the engineer's assignments.

Sincerely,

Richard

In this case Richard needs a response and has told Susan exactly what he wants: her approval to transfer an engineer and a computer.

One major problem with requests and proposals is that writers tend to tell when they need to sell. For example, Carol Winters, a manufacturing manager, wants to correct the problem of traffic flow into the plant which causes traffic jams and parking shortages. She suggests staggering lunch hours between shifts. Here's the first email she wrote:

Dear Shift Supervisors:

Starting May 28, please delay the start of Shift A lunch hour to 12:30 p.m.

Sincerely,

Carol

Although her message is clear and concise, some shift operators might resist the change because they don't understand *why* she's making this request. Because she needs their cooperation for her plan to work, she has to make sure the supervisors fully understand what she is trying to accomplish. Here is the revised email:

Dear Shift Supervisors:

To avoid traffic jams and parking issues during the lunch hour, I propose that we stagger Shift A's lunch hour. Starting May 28, please delay the start of Shift A lunch hour to 12:30 p.m. Please call me by May 21 if this causes a problem for you.

Sincerely,

Carol

Carol's first attempt is informative but not very convincing: it *tells*. Her second attempt tries to get the readers on her side and is much more likely to persuade them to accept her proposal. It *sells*.

Decide What the Reader Needs to Know

Knowing how much your reader already knows about the topic provides a starting point for your communications. When Emily Chan wrote to contract employees to inform them that they were to be included in the company pension plan, she was able to start with a direct statement:

The Executive Committee has agreed to extend the company pension plan to all contract employees.

In this case Emily knew that contract employees had already been previously informed that the extension had been proposed, so she wasn't delivering unexpected news. She also knew that the other readers, such as permanent employees (who, though not directly addressed, might see her email), would also not be surprised by the news because the company had also kept them informed of the proposed change, even though it did not affect them.

If the company had worked behind the scenes in preparing this proposal and had not kept the employees informed, Emily's announcement would have come as a surprise. In that case she would have had to build some background information into her email:

Dear Contract Employees,

Since its inception in 2002, Vancourt Business Systems' pension plan has applied only to permanent employees. I am pleased to announce that shortly it will also apply to contract employees. The Executive Committee has agreed to extend the company pension plan to all contract employees.

If, like Emily, you know your readers reasonably well, you can easily establish how much they already know about your topic. However, if you do not know your readers, or if there are multiple readers (which with today's standards of forwarding messages, it's very likely there are) you must decide how much information you need to provide. Without doing this preliminary work, you are likely to have difficulty finding the correct starting point for your audience(s). Understanding who your readers are, what they already know, and what they need to know will help focus your writing and eliminate much of the unnecessary background information that can clutter your letters, reports, proposals, emails, and text messages.

Here are important guidelines to help you decide what information you must include. First, divide your information into two groups:

Need to know   These are the details that the reader *must* have to fully understand the situation (in a *tell* message) or to make a decision (in a *sell* message).

Nice to know   These are the less important details that *may* interest the reader but are not necessary to fully understand the situation or to make a decision.

Next, focus your communication by presenting only the "**need to know**" details.

An Introduction to The Pyramid Method of Writing™

Once you have identified who you are writing to and what the purpose of your communication is, you need to organize your information into a logical, easy-to-understand order. Earlier in this chapter we introduced you to the idea of dividing information into two compartments: the Summary Statement and the Supporting Details.

The **Summary Statement** tells the reader what he or she most wants to know, or needs to be told, but only in general terms.

The **Supporting Details** compartment provides specific details that support or expand on what you said in the Summary Statement, this time in concrete terms.

Notice how, in Figure 1-6, the information visually forms a pyramid, with the Summary Statement at the top. This reinforces the idea that the Summary Statement should be brief, so it will fit into the small space.

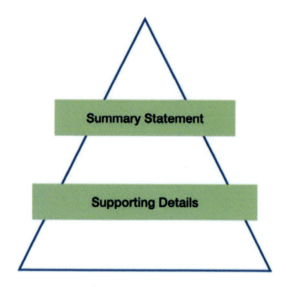

Figure 1-6: The basic Pyramid structure

Expanding the Supporting Details

Once you have written the Summary Statement, you need to consider the impact it will have on your readers and anticipate the questions they may have after reading it. What will they want to know? You can start by asking yourself six basic questions: Who? What? When? Where? Why? and How? You may not have to answer all six questions, just those that apply to the situation you are writing about. You answer these questions in the Supporting Details compartment.

To help organize the information logically, figure 1-7 shows how the **Supporting Details** compartment is divided into three sub-compartments.

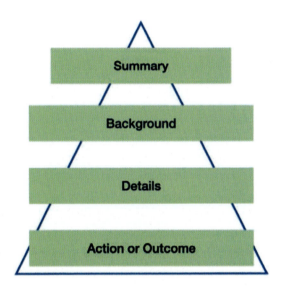

Figure 1-7: Expanding the supporting details

Everything you write in these compartments must support or relate to the information you write in the **Summary Statement**.

The **Background** compartment sets the scene for the details that follow it and answers the questions:

Who was involved?
When did this happen?
Where did this happen?
Why did this happen?

The **Details** compartment provides all of the information the reader needs to understand the current status of the project, as in a progress report. This compartment also helps the reader come to a conclusion, make a decision, or give approval, as in a request or proposal. The Details compartment answers the questions:

What has happened or is happening?
What effect has this had, and *what* has been done about it?
Why did this happen?, and
How did this happen? In some cases explaining the "how" may not be
necessary—it might be more information than your reader needs to know.

The **Outcome/Action** compartment answers the questions:

What is the result?
What has to be done, by *when*? And by *whom*?

Depending on whether you are writing a tell or a sell message, this last
compartment label will vary. For instance, a tell document has an **Outcome**
compartment because that last sub-compartment only describes *results*, events
that have occurred and actions that have already been taken.

A sell document has an **Action** compartment because it identifies who has to act
or react (often the reader), and what action that person has to take.

The labels assigned to each compartment are not used as heading in a short
email, or report, although they may appear in a longer document or a formal
report.

In the letter to an electronics supplier shown in Figure 1-8, the four writing
compartments are clearly defined. Notice how short, direct, and easy to read the
letter is when the Pyramid Method of Writing™ is used.

Summary Statement

Background

Details

Action

Dear Mr. Ashe:

The video surveillance camera we purchased from you has failed for the third time this year. This time I am requesting that you replace it rather than repair it.

It is the Exalta Model 100B and was one of a four-part security system we purchased for our store. We ordered it from you on purchase order M2327 dated February 12, 2020, and which you supplied on invoice 09213, dated February 23, 2020. Since then, the camera has been repaired twice.

The first failure occurred on April 12, 2020, two months after the initial purchase and one month after the warranty had expired. Repairs at your store cost $65.25.

Five months later, on September 21, 2020, the same camera broke again. This cost 87.50 to repair (see invoice 09452).

Yesterday, October 14, 2020, it failed a third time.

To date we have incurred $152.75 in repair costs; that's almost half of the original price, on a camera that is only eight months old. Consequently, I am asking you to send a replacement camera by November 15 at no cost to us. You may send it care of me to our business at 5784 Harcourt Road, Atlanta, Georgia, 30306.

Regards,

Jonathan Kelly
Manager

Figure 1-8: A letter using the Pyramid Method of Writing™

Chapter 2

WRITING SHORT CORRESPONDENCES

It's surprising how much time people spend writing in their everyday work. Did you know, for example, that electrical engineers have reported that up to 80% of their week is spent communicating and a big part of that is in writing? This includes writing emails, text messages, reports and other forms of documentation. They complain that in college they avoided English classes because they didn't like to write, and now, that's all they seem to do!

Writing Good News and Bad News

Mark is struggling with a letter he needs to write to a client. He is responsible for telling them that his company has not accepted their credit and that the contract work cannot start. He felt the Pyramid Method™ was too abrupt for sending bad news. He had been taught that if you have to deliver bad news, bury it at the end, after you've explained all the reasons why something is bad. Figure 2-1 shows his first attempt, in which he reverted to the climactic way of writing.

Dear Mr. Boland:

Thank you for submitting your paperwork so promptly to the Genesee Savings and Loan for review. We are looking forward to working with you in building your house and specifically to installing the kitchen you designed at our offices. I'm particularly pleased with your decision to go with the higher quality materials.

As we discussed during our last meeting, I am your contact person at Kreative Kitchens and Design and will be responsible for overseeing all of the work in your new home. The cabinets and countertops have already been ordered and the styles and colours that you requested are available. We had expected delivery to the house within four weeks. Unfortunately, we can't confirm that they will be delivered until your finances are approved.

Mary Jane Dougherty from the Genesee Savings and Loan has just informed me that your loan application was not approved. This causes a problem with our supplier. Without the proper financing they not only will not deliver the supplies, but they also will not guarantee the supplies' availability.

I'm sorry to break this news to you and hope you can resolve this situation soon so we can continue with our original plan; otherwise, the completion date will need to be adjusted.

Sincerely,

Mark Mathews

Account Manager

Figure 2-1: A bad news letter that does not use the Pyramid Method™

Mark's letter would have been clearer and more concise if he had used the Pyramid Method™ and put a Summary Statement at the beginning. His revised letter is shown in Figure 2-2.

Dear Mr. Boland:

Mary Jane Dougherty from the Genesee Savings and Loan has just informed me that your loan application was not approved. This causes a problem with our supplier. Without the proper financing they will not deliver the supplies, and they also will not guarantee them.

As we discussed during our last meeting, I am your contact person at Kreative Kitchens and Design and will oversee all of the work in your new home. The cabinets and countertops have already been ordered and the styles and colours that you requested are available. We can expect delivery to the house within four weeks of your financial approval. Unfortunately, we can't confirm delivery until your finances are approved.

I'm sorry to break this news to you and hope you can resolve this situation soon so we can continue with our original plan; otherwise, the completion date will need to be adjusted. As soon as I receive notice of your finances being approved, I will confirm the order with our supplier.

Sincerely,

Mark Mathews

Account Manager

Figure 2-2: A bad news letter using the Pyramid Method™

In Mark's revised letter, Mr. Boland immediately understands the problem and what he needs to do. He also knows what action Mark will take. The letter is shorter, more concise, and creates a confident image of the writer.

Whether you are delivering good or bad news, put the Summary Statement right up front and then follow it with all the Supporting Details.

Types of Letters

Many software programs or web sites offer templates and samples of emails, letters, or memos you can edit. Be careful: it is extremely important that your letters "sound" like you. It's also very important that you use the Pyramid Method™, and many of these do not. We want you to develop your own style and know how to organize your own thoughts into coherent messages. This section discusses some typical and most used communication situations and describes the associated writing plans. Remember that the Pyramid Method™ is flexible, and if you don't see your exact situation here, you can easily develop your own pyramid using the techniques you are learning.

Writing Complaint Letters

Every day people experience problems with equipment they purchased, services they've sought, or situations they encounter and they need to explain the situation to the vendor, manufacturer, or a person in charge. Others discover errors made in orders, billing, charges, or other forms of payment. In these situations, people have a complaint and they need something done to resolve the situation. Sometimes they can make a complaint in person or via an online video media, but more often than not, people first attempt to resolve the complaint in writing. If you follow our principles, this can be very effective and your complaint can be quickly resolved without any face-to-face communication.

A complaint letter must be firm and definite without sounding abrasive. No matter how upset a person is, emotion won't get the issue resolved. Facts will. So, the person with the complaint must present the facts clearly and definitively, so the reader can readily identify the problem and what action is required to resolve it. If a complaint shows too much anger or is abusive, he or she will likely create resistance from the reader. See Chapter 6 for information on choosing the right words and avoiding words that might provoke a reader.

Figure 2-3 shows the pyramid for a complaint letter. It breaks the information into four compartments:

Figure 2-3: Writing Pyramid for a complaint letter

1. The **Summary** Statement, which has two parts:

    a. It identifies what the problem is.
    b. It states the action desired from the reader.

These parts may be combined into a single sentence or broken into two:

Dear Ms. Wahl:

The customized microchips you supplied to us on February 15 were not exactly as ordered, so we are requesting a price-reduction.

The Summary Statement offers generalizations rather than specific details because more exact information will follow later in the letter. Make sure it always contains both the problem *and* a requested action.

2. The **Background** describes the circumstances affecting the complaint and lists the numbers and dates of associated documents:

We ordered them on our purchase order No. 2463 on January 6 and supplied on your invoice No. 4390 dated February 11.

In a short letter, you can combine the Background compartment with either the Summary Statement or the Complaint Details compartment to form a single paragraph.

3.   The **Complaint Details** compartment describes exactly what went wrong.

We requested 2000 sets of type 37412 chips, but when the order arrived, we found you sent type 37812 chips instead.

4.   The **Action** compartment identifies what the writer wants the reader to do to correct the problems.

Rather than destroy the chips, we have chosen to keep them. We request that you credit our account with the difference between the price of 2000 sets of type 37412 and 37812. We also request that you send us 2000 sets of the 37412 chips and do not charge us a shipping fee, since we have kept and paid for an extra, unscheduled order. Please confirm by May 22 when you will ship the new order and that you will not charge us shipping.

The Action compartment must be absolutely clear, firm, and purposeful. There should be no doubt in the reader's mind what the writer wants done.

The four writing compartments are clearly defined in this next email to a credit card company, see in Figure 2-4. This is another example of a complaint and a request for adjustment. Use this structure for any complaint message you may need to send.

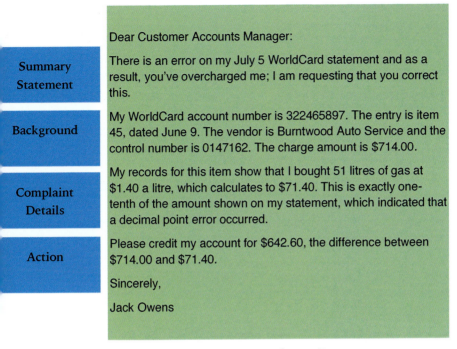

Summary Statement

Background

Complaint Details

Action

Dear Customer Accounts Manager:

There is an error on my July 5 WorldCard statement and as a result, you've overcharged me; I am requesting that you correct this.

My WorldCard account number is 322465897. The entry is item 45, dated June 9. The vendor is Burntwood Auto Service and the control number is 0147162. The charge amount is $714.00.

My records for this item show that I bought 51 litres of gas at $1.40 a litre, which calculates to $71.40. This is exactly one-tenth of the amount shown on my statement, which indicated that a decimal point error occurred.

Please credit my account for $642.60, the difference between $714.00 and $71.40.

Sincerely,

Jack Owens

Figure 2-4: A request for adjustment

This is a good example of a situation in which writing an email is best. Neither a text message nor a phone or video call will allow you to document the needed detail.

Writing Request Letters

Whether you are requesting funding for new equipment, additional staff or to attend a conference or course, you need to write your request so that the person who needs to approve it can base his or her decision on facts that are presented clearly and coherently. Too often people approach the decision makers in person and bombard them with facts and figures. It is unreasonable to expect someone to allocate funding based on a discussion. We suggest you briefly present the request in person (if possible) and then follow your discussion with the details in a concise written message. Your efforts will be appreciated and will allow the decision maker time to thoroughly review the information. Without time to review all the facts, a decision maker is more likely to deny the request.

Figure 2-5 shows the writing compartments for a request or short proposal. They are similar to those for a complaint.

1.   The Summary briefly describes your request and asks for approval.
2.   The Background or Reason, describes the circumstances leading up to your request, and establishes why the request is important (in very short requests, the Summary Statement and Reason are often combined into a single paragraph.)
3.   The Request Details describe in detail

•   what the request entails,

•   what will be gained if the request is granted,

•   what problems may be created if the request is approved, and how you plan to overcome them, and

•   what the cost will be, financially and to the organization's resources (personnel and material).

4.   An Action Statement clearly identifies what you want the reader to do after he or she has read your request.

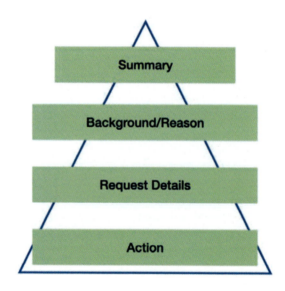

Figure 2-5: Writing pyramid for a request or short proposal

The message in Figure 2-6 shows how a request can also be a proposal. Note that in this example,

- the Summary Statement and the Reason are in the same paragraph,

- there is both a Reason *and* a Background,

- the Background and Details are in the same paragraph, and

- the Action Statement states both what the writer wants the reader to do, and what action the writer will take.

This demonstrates the flexibility you have when using the writing compartments. Whether a single paragraph embraces two compartments or several paragraphs comprise a single compartment is unimportant as *long as you keep them in the correct sequence.*

February 11

Dear Ms Yaremeko:

Summary Statement- Reason

I am requesting your approval to change the dates of our monthly preventive maintenance service for your Rotomat extruders and shapers to the 29th of each month. This will help spread my technicians' workload more evenly and will provide you with better service.

Background

Our contract with you is No. RE208 dated January 4 and it requires that we perform monthly inspections and maintenance on the 15th day of each month. Unfortunately, almost all of our clients ask that we perform their maintenance service between the 5th and the 25th, so that we don't overlap the month-end. This creates a problem for us in that our service technicians experience a peak workload for 20 days and then have very little work for 10 days.

Request Details

Will you please let me know by February 25 if you accept this change? I will send a technician to your shop on February 28 for a second visit this month, rather than create a six-week space between the February and March inspections. There will be no charge for this extra service.

Action

Sincerely,

Tony DeCarlo

Figure 2-6: A request or proposal message

Writing a Reference

You may be asked by someone who has worked for you or with you to write a letter of reference for them. Such messages may be required for employment reasons, to accompany a university or college application, or to gain membership to a professional society.

When someone asks you to write a reference on his or her behalf, try to find out how the reference will be used so that what you write can be tailored to the situation. Whenever possible find out the name of the person to address it to or at least the name of the company or organization. This avoids starting with impersonal words like "To Whom it May Concern". Readers understand that these words are generic and non-direct and seem less credible than those addressed directly to a person. If you don't know who you are writing to, then write to a position:

Dear Human Resource Manager
Dear Potential Employer of Andrew Smith
Dear Selection Committee

There are certain facts that a prospective employer or evaluation committee want to hear from you, and they must be built into a fairly short message. They include, but are not limited to (and not necessarily in this order):

- who you are,

- the connection between you and the person you are writing,

- the quality of work or service performed by the person you are writing about, and

- special attributes the person has which the *reader* would find valuable.

You should also anticipate the question, "If the opportunity presented itself, would you hire this person?" For example, you might write:

If Briana Jones ever decides to reapply to us for employment, we would welcome her application.

Figure 2-7 shows the pyramid for a reference. It breaks the information into three compartments:

1. The Summary identifies the person and briefly comments on his or her main qualities.

2. The Evidence compartment supports what is said in the Summary Statement and gives additional information about the person that is useful and relevant. Specific details are particularly important because they increase credibility of the content.

Janet was employed with us for several years.

This sentence creates a vague or wishy-washy impression. Be specific:

Janet was employed as a service representative for three years and a traffic supervisor for two years.

Refer to the person by his or her first name rather than last name (Jane, instead of Ms. Smith), because it will help create the impression that you know the person well and are therefore in a good position to give accurate comments.

3. The Closing Statement offers a final comment which can either sum up the person's capabilities or be a more personal statement:

Janet was a responsible, well-motivated employee. I wish her well in all that she does.

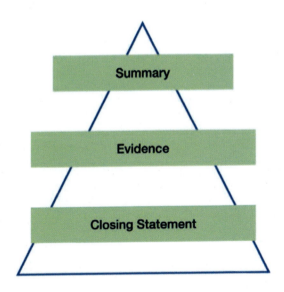

Figure 2-7: Writing pyramid for a reference

What do you do if you are asked to give a reference for a person who was not a good worker or whose interpersonal skills were poor and caused friction with other employees? You can't honestly give a glowing reference because if the person is hired based on your recommendation and proves to be inadequate, your credibility would be placed in doubt. You have two alternatives:

1. If an individual you are doubtful about asks for a reference, politely decline.
2. If an employer asks you directly for a reference for a person, you can keep it very short and comment briefly on his or her positive aspects, with little or no elaboration.

Figure 2-8 is an example of a reference letter.

Dear Potential Employer:

I'm pleased to recommend Matt Jacobs as a qualified and competent pilot to your organization. He possesses both the necessary skills and experience to succeed.

As a realtor and businesswoman, I was a student of Matt's for six months. I've known him for 18 months. During that time, I was able to observe him not only as a flight instructor but also as a member of the community. He is loyal, patient, dependable, flexible, and has excellent judgment.

Through my flight instruction he met my two young boys and always made an extra effort to accommodate their needs. They are both in wheelchairs and Matt's sensitivity and perception were admirable. He still corresponds with the boys. I could always count on Matt to be early to our appointments and he made sure he was there for me in my timeframe. He understood and appreciated the time constraints I have with my personal and professional commitments.

I never doubted Matt's abilities or judgement because I always felt secure with him in the plane. More than once he altered the flight pattern and route for safety reasons. For a student, practicing safety is an invaluable lesson – for a commercial pilot, it is a requirement. Rarely do you see such confidence in a young man of Matt's age.

In my realty business I meet people with various backgrounds and personalities and I consider myself an excellent judge of character. I have never seen a finer young man than Matt Jacobs and know that whatever he chooses to do in life he will give it 100% and be a success.

Sincerely,

Barbara Johnson

Figure 2-8: A reference letter

Writing an Instruction

You may have to provide directions to your staff, clients, colleagues, or vendors

or explain to a new employee how to access the company's computer system. When providing instructions, it is particularly important that your writing is clear, concise, and complete. The language you use will establish the reader's confidence in both your instructions and their abilities. Your words must be direct, concise, and accurate.

Figure 2-9 shows the writing pyramid for an instruction. It has four compartments. Typically, an Action Statement is unnecessary because the communication is informative.

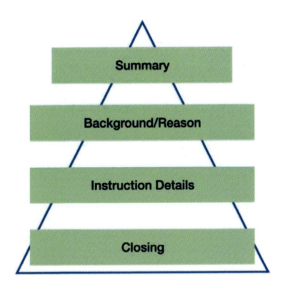

Figure 2-9: Writing Pyramid for an instruction

1. The Summary Statement describes very briefly what has to be done.

2. Including a Reason is important because readers more readily follow instructions when they understand why such instructions are necessary. For example, if the instructions explain that the reason for taking a different travel route is to avoid delays, the reader understands why they need to

follow the instructions. Frequently, the Reason is stated in the same paragraph as the Summary Statement and the other Background begins a new paragraph.

3.   The Instruction Details are the steps the reader must follow. Guidelines for writing the steps follow.

•   Keep each step short so the reader does not have to wade through a lengthy paragraph to find out what needs to be one. This also helps the reader remember the details while he or she performs the task.

•   Start each step with an active verb, such as *connect, position, calculate*, or *deliver*. Action verbs make your instructions sound authoritative and give readers confidence in you as the instruction giver and in their ability to carry out the task.

•   Number each step consecutively if the sequence is essential. Also use numbers if you are showing priority or have to refer back to an item, otherwise, bullets are appropriate.

•   Quote specific details rather than generalizations, particularly avoiding ambiguous words such as about, should, near, and close to.

4.   The Closing Statement replaces the Outcome/Action compartment because it simply wraps up the communication using positive language.

Figure 2-10 shows an instruction communication with a clear and definite tone.

Summary Statement-Reason	To: Morgan Paulsen From: Marita Estavo We have just received a large order that is going to put considerate pressure on the Production Department. Delivery dates are extremely tight, which means you will have to set up the line quickly if the first 100 units are to be shipped on schedule.
Background	The order is the 300 BLS-201 modular interactive learning systems and the client is Tormont Education Systems Limited (see attached purchase order).
Instruction Details	Because the first 100 units must be delivered by May 6, we need to complete the following steps: 1. Count the existing stock of system components. 2. Place orders with suppliers today for immediate delivery of additional components to complete the first 100 units.

3. Work out a schedule showing completion dates for parts acquisition, assembly, packing and shipping.

4. Place follow-up orders with suppliers for delivery of the components for the remaining 200 units.

5. Inform the system assemblers that they may have to work overtime between April 20 and May 6.

6. Forewarn the shipping department workers that they will need to create 100 packing cartons one week in advance of the delivery date.

Closing Statement

I don't foresee any problems in meeting the scheduled deadlines. Call me if you encounter any issues.

Figure 2-10: An instruction communication

Some General Writing Guidelines to Consider

Regardless of the type of communication you are writing, there are some effective general business practices to use.

Balance the page

Spread out the content of your communication using extra line breaks between paragraphs to help create a more attractive visual presence. One large block of text is distracting as is too much white space if the text is all in the top third of page when printed.

Address your audience

In business communications, use "Dear" to set a professional tone. If you don't know the person, write to a position: "Dear Customer Service Manager" rather than "To whom it may concern". The trend today is to be informal and move to the first person as soon as possible "Dear Lauren" or simply "Lauren" if you work closely with the person. We suggest you use the more formal greeting "Dear Ms. Santos" if you are addressing a new client or if sending it to multiple readers who might not know you. Once you have established a relationship you can move to the more informal, first name.

The use of a colon (:) or comma (,) after the greeting is optional. Be consistent. If you use punctuation after the greeting, then use it after the closing too.

Identify yourself

Always add your name at the end of the communication and provide your contact details. In an email, type your name in addition to the signature file, which provides your contact information.

Use standard margins and fonts

Most readers expect a 1 in. margin on all sides of the printed text, but to balance the page vertically, you may have to adjust this. Avoid narrowing the margins to make the text fit into one page because it makes the line length too long for the eye. Choose a simple common font and appropriate size. Typically, 10-11 point is readable in most fonts. See Chapter 5, Customizing Your Documents.

Reference any attachments or enclosures

If you attach a document, refer to it so the reader knows it is there. "See the attached invoice C5603 for more detail".

Close professionally

There are only two acceptable closings for professional business communications: "Sincerely" or "Regards". Follow these with your name. In emails insert a signature file afterwards which contains your full name, position, organization, and contact information.

Avoid signing off with "Thanks", "Thank you", or "Thanking you in advance". If you always say Thanks, your readers won't know when you really are offering a true thanks after they have done something deserving.

Proofread

You must proofread every communication very carefully. Your writing is projecting an image of you, your company, and the content and if you have typos, unorganized thoughts, or poor sentence structure and grammar, you are presenting a sloppy, careless image. We encourage you to print your documents and edit on the physical page; you'll catch more of the issues this way than reading online.

Understand the grammar tools your software offers and make sure you check the settings.

Use the Pyramid Method of Writing™

All of your communications must be clear, concise, and complete. Use the structured method we present in this book to organize your content and make it easier for your reader.

1. Start with what you most want your reader to know and, if appropriate, what action you want the reader to take.
2. Follow with any Supporting Details the reader may need to understand the reason for your message, and provide information about any point that may need further explanation.

Check that each message contains only the information your reader will need to be informed or to respond, and no more. Be conscious to separate the essential *need to know* information from the less important *nice to know* details.

Some General Guidelines for Writing Emails

"Netiquette" means "the etiquette of communicating on the internet" and although there are not established rules or procedures, we offer the following considerations to ensure you are an effective communicator.

Remember that email and texts are just two tools you have to send a message and may not always be the best media. Nothing replaces the value of face-to-face communication but often the phone or video platforms might help. When choosing to send an email, make it a conscious decision and in addition to the guidelines we already addressed, consider these email-specific guidelines.

Use proper language

Often we are typing or texting quickly which can lead to us being careless. Just because it is considered a fast and often informal tool it doesn't mean you can write short, cryptic messages: "Yes", "I don't think so" are not complete thoughts.

Use proper punctuation and full sentences to help your reader understand your information. An incomplete sentence may cause confusion or misinformation. Being too concise risks being clear and complete.

The words you choose and the length of your sentences set a certain tone. Don't be abrupt, or use too many short sentences and don't hide behind the technology and write something you would never say in person to your audience.

Use direct subject lines

The subject line of an email is the first clue to your audience as to what the message is about. Make it relevant and meaningful to your audience. Subjects like "Forwarded Message", "Questions" or "Help" don't encourage the reader to open the message and read it. Some people will check the sender's name to see if they recognize it to decide which messages need attention first. If they don't know you, then they rely on your subject line.

Use the Pyramid Method of Writing™

Even in short email communications, use the Pyramid Method™ to structure your content. The first sentence of your email should let your reader know the situation and if there is something they need to do after reading the message.

Be professional and ethical

Remember that email and texts are not good tools for conveying confidential information and uncomplimentary remarks about others. Electronic messages can too easily be forwarded or copied to other people and then you have no control over who else might see what you have written. Be just as professional in email and text as you would be with all other types of business communications. Your company or organization "owns" your communications.

Emoticons or emojis are not professional and do not belong in business communications. Someone in your audience may not understand it or find it offensive. You also could be seen as immature.

Stick to Need to Know information only

In our fast-paced business environments, your audience is reading your content to understand or to decide. Provide only the information they *need to know*. Email is not the best tool for building rapport or bonding; use the phone, video or in person. Be clear, concise, and complete and your audience will appreciate your useful messages.

Consider multiple readers

If you are writing to multiple readers, consider different people may have different content needs and level of understanding. In some cases it might be more productive to send two messages rather than one single, all-embracing email.

Write
1. a short summary, which you send to readers who are interested only in the main event and the result, and
2. a detailed message, which you send to readers who need all of the specifics.

You can also accomplish this with the summary as the email message and the specifics as an attachment.

Avoid "Reply All"

Be selective when relying to a multiple-reader email or text. It may be tempting and easy to simply click "Reply All" rather than take the time to address your reply to only those readers who need it. Because it goes to everyone on the original list others may follow and reply back to everyone. This practice creates far too many messages and wastes people's time and focus.

Move messages out of In Box

Avoid letting messages accumulate for too long in your In Box. If you want to keep a message or refer to it later, move it into a project folder or Action Item folder. Periodically review your In Box and folders to see what you can delete. Old meeting agendas and minutes clutter up your filing system.

When replying insert parts of original message

When replying to a message, consider quoting a line or two from the original message to help put your response into perspective. This takes the most pertinent information from the original message and allows you to just address that point. Use some formatting to identify the excerpt and your response:

Dan Singh wrote on May 12:
>> The Society's constitution was last updated in 2013 and needs amending.

LM: I agree, but first we need to check how much editing Karen Ellsberg did in 2019.

Insert your name before your signature file

Consider the signature file the same as a business card that identifies your full name, company, position, email, phone, and website. To help personalize your communication, simply add your name.

Sincerely,
Lori

Lori Marra
Senior Consultant
RGI International, Inc.
www.rgilearning.com

Avoid emotionally charged responses

If you are annoyed or irritated by a message you receive, wait before replying so you won't regret sending a message written in the haste of an emotional moment. Let your irritation or frustration cool down. Email is for transmitting facts and is the wrong tool for handling conflicts.

Use simple formatting

If your message has tables and visuals, attaching a protected PDF document will ensure the formatting is retained and the reader can use the file rather than have it in the email software.

Keep your fonts standard and avoid large graphics. Many people are accessing and reading emails on small devices with possibly limited bandwidth or signals.

Chapter 3

WRITING SHORT REPORTS

Why write reports? Mangers in a well-run company need to be fed a continual stream of information about what is happening in their departments. This does not mean a manager's role is simply to act as a watchdog, keeping an eye on every employee and checking that everyone is doing their job properly. Rather it means that each manager needs to know what is being done for each task, what problems have affected work progress, and whether the problems will cause a delay in a particular projects' planned completion date. Mangers use this information to plan future work, to assign additional staff to a task, to predict operating costs, to develop a budget for future activities, and to report profitability to the company's executives.

As a report writer, the information that you provide can vary. For example, you might have to describe the results of a meeting you held with a client, or a power outage that stopped production on an assembly line and ruined a set of tests you were conducting, or what progress has been made on a software program you are developing for a client.

You may pass some of this information on to your supervisor by word of mouth, present a report as an activity update to a group at a department meeting, or prepare a short written report to your peers. In each case your report should evolve from the writing pyramids described in Chapter 2. The next two chapters show how the writing compartments can be expanded and adapted to suit each situation and the information you have to convey.

Types of Short Reports

A hospital nurse working the night shift has to leave a note for the ward supervisor (who works the day shift) to inform her that the respirator was knocked over during the night and must be sent out for repair. A designer has to describe to an architect how his CAD designs are progressing. A sales executive needs to explain what happened during a meeting at a client site. A plumber installing toilets in a new high-rise apartment block has to inform the building contractor that the holes cut in the eighth floor of the building are too small to accept the pipe chosen for the job, that she has spent extra time enlarging the holes, and that she will have to charge for the extra work she has done. A project manager has to explain the lessons learned during the 13-month development cycle of new processing equipment.

All five have a message to *tell:*

- The nurse has to *tell* the ward supervisor...

- The designer has to *describe* progress to the architects...

- The sales executive has to *explain* to the management team...

- The plumber needs to *inform* the contractor...

- The project manager has to *explain* to the other project managers...

Each of these reports deals with facts. The writers have to *tell* their readers about something that has happened or is currently happening. There are five types of reports:

1. To report an event or accident

You write an incident report (the nurse).

2. To report what was done during a field assignment (on a job that was done away from your regular place of work)

You write a field report (the sale executive).

3. To report on the condition of a location, building, or equipment,

You write an inspection report (the plumber).

4. To describe how a job is progressing (for a project that is not yet complete),

You write a progress report (the designer).

5. To describe a job or task that is finished,

You write a project completion report (the project manager).

This chapter describes all five reports and how you can use the Pyramid or adapt it to your unique situation.

Reporting an Event or Incident

An incident report uses the same pyramid structure we presented in Chapter 2. Figure 3-1 shows it has the same four-compartment writing plan. Only one label changes:

1. The Summary Statement briefly describes the incident and its main effects.
2. The Background describes the circumstances leading up to the incident. It describes who was involved and when and where the incident occurred.
3. The Event covers the incident (the what happened), with more specifics and details than in the Summary Statement.
4. The Outcome identifies factors evolving from the event, discusses their implications, and describes what actions you have taken as a result of the incident.

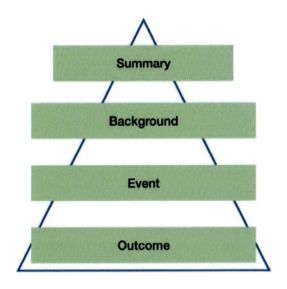

Figure 3-1: Writing Pyramid for an incident report

The length of an incident report can vary from being very short to moderately long, depending partly on the size and effect of the Event, and partly on the amount of information the reader needs to fully understand the Event and its effects. It can be as simple as a single sentence:

On May 27, in our Regent Avenue plant, a fire caused a one-day loss of production.

Here, the Background is:

On May 27 in our Regent Avenue plant,...

The Event is:
a fire...

And the Outcome, or result is:
caused a one-day loss of production.

For most readers such a basic statement would be inadequate. If you were a company executive, you would expect a much more detailed report: one similar to that in Figure 3-2.

Summary Statement

Background

Event

To: Vern Rampersaad, Vice President

From: Sheen Walters, Personnel Supervisor

Date: January 21

Ref: Work stoppage at Regent Avenue

A fire has caused a one-day loss of production at our Regent Avenue plant.

The incident occurred at 8:45 a.m. on Monday January 20. The fire started in the kitchen of The Stepp Inn Café, which is housed in the same building and is immediately adjacent to our assembly line test station.

The fire was caused when the handle on a pail of cooking oil broke as the pail was being lifted onto the stove. The oil spilled onto the burners and ignited immediately.

When the fire department arrived at 8:57 a.m. the fire chief ordered a complete evacuation of the building. The fire was extinguished by 10:30 a.m.

The fire completely gutted The Stepp Inn and burned a 1.30 m diameter hole through the wall separating the café from our offices. Our assembly line test station received considerable smoke and water damage. Because of the smoke and fumes that permeated the building, the fire chief did not permit staff to re-enter the building until 6:15 p.m.

I have instructed ARC Builders Ltd. to install a temporary wall at the east end of the building, in front of the fire-damaged wall. The temporary wall will be completed overnight. I have also rented air extractors to remove the fumes.

Outcome

The work stoppage will put us one day behind schedule with our contract to assemble modules for the Krypton Corporation.

Figure 3-2: An incident report using the Pyramid Method™

In a very short report, a single paragraph may cover more than one compartment. For example, the following paragraph covers both the Summary Statement and the Background:

The May 19 inspection of microwave tower No. 14 shows that the transmission line on the vertical riser is frayed and needs to be replaced.

In a long incident report, each writing compartment may contain several paragraphs (as the Event compartment does in Figure 3-2). When a report is long, it's a good idea to introduce each writing compartment with a heading. Although you could use Background, Event, and Outcome as headings, try to create headings that better represent the content. For the fire damage report in Figure 3-2, for example,

To Introduce	You could use this heading
The Background	Location of Fire
The Event	Extent of Fire
The Outcome	Post-fire Action

Reporting a Field Trip

Whenever you return from a field trip, you will be expected to write a brief report describing what you saw, what you did, and sometimes, what still needs to be done. (A field trip is anytime you are away from your normal work environment.) This applies just as much to a one-hour visit to a local computer distributor for a product demonstration as it does to a three-week stay at a paper mill during which you and two other team members replace old wiring and install a new control panel. The report you write should describe your impressions (of the computer product) or provide a detailed account of the work that was done (at the paper mill). You should submit a written report rather than as a spoken report partly because you shouldn't trust your memory to remember details several months after the assignment. A written report is essential mostly because your company will need a permanent record of what was done and to help technicians who visit the site and work with the same equipment or people in the future.

The four writing compartments for a field trip report are shown in Figure 3-3.

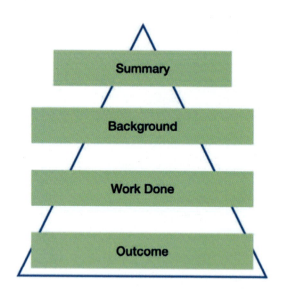

Figure 3-3: Writing pyramid for a field trip report

1. In the Summary Statement briefly describe where you went and what you did or achieved, and comment on the trip's outcome.
2. In the Background, provide information about the assignment, and answer the questions, who went where, when and why? For example:

Who?	Wes Freeman and I visited the
Where?	Whinney Lake monitoring station
When?	On July 17-18
Why?	To carry out annual maintenance of the automatic water level measuring equipment.

You may also include information such as the name of the person authorizing the trip, the type of transportation you used (personal or company vehicle, commercial flight, or chartered helicopter), and the names of people you worked with or contacted at the job site.

In a very short trip report you may combine the Background with the Summary.

3. In the Work Done compartment, describe what you did while at the job site or on the field assignment. This can range from a short description of a routine test of a radio transmitter and receiver, to a long narrative pointing out problems with the transmitter and describing unscheduled work you had to carry out to make it work.

In a longer report, we suggest you break this compartment into three subcompartments, as shown in Figure 3-4:

    a. Write about **Planned Work** or routine work very briefly. If possible, refer to an instruction sheet or maintenance procedure rather than mention all the details of the work that was done.

    b. Cover unusual or **Unplanned Work** in more detail, because it will be new to the reader. State what you did, why you did it that way, and what the results were.

    c. Explain the **Problems Encountered** in detail, so readers understand the factors that made the job more difficult than expected and, if necessary, what steps should be taken to prevent the problems from happening again.

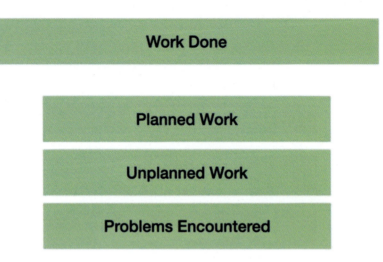

Figure 3-4: Subcompartments of work done

4. In the Outcome compartment, comment on the main achievement(s) or result(s) of your trip and draw attention to any work that you could not do or finish. If possible, suggest how, when, and by whom the work should be done or complete. A short informal field trip report is shown in Figure 3-5.

Hilary

Summary and Background

My examination of the Rega model 301 bread-slicing machine shows it would be a good choice for our bakery. I examined the 301 in operation on October 20 at Modern Bakeries' Main Street plant, at the invitation of MB's production assistant George Fey.

Work Done

The Rega 301 is fast, efficient, and extremely safe. It fully lives up to the manufacturer's claims in the attached advertising sheet. Mr. Fey said that it regularly slices 2700 loaves per hour, which is 20% faster than our machine. They have two Rega 301s and have had no breakdowns in the seven months they have been in operation. The 301's positive safety features are particularly attractive.

Outcome

I am convinced this is the right machine for our bakery and recommend we budget $16,000 to buy three next year.

Nancy

Figure 3-5: A short field trip report

Reporting Course or Conference Attendance

You can use the field trip writing pyramid to describe the results of a course or conference you have attended by changing the Work Done compartment to Course/Conference Details. Figure 3-6 shows the four writing compartments.

1. In the Summary Statement, state what course or conference you attended and the main impact it had on you. For example:

To: Vince Warchuk, Manager Human Resources Department

The *Making Effective Oral Presentations* seminar I attended presented useful information and provided ample opportunities for practice. I suggest we bring the seminar in-house for other supervisors.

2. In the Background answer the questions *Who? When? Where? Why?*:

The seminar was presented by Joan Porter-Farr of Presentations International of Toronto. It was held at the Norfolk Hotel from 9 a.m. to 4:30 p.m. and the cost was $235 per person. There were 12 participants, which is the maximum recommended to ensure individual attention for each participant.

3. In the Course/Conference Details compartment, identify the topics you want to discuss. We suggest choosing topics from the following list:

- Identify your expectation or objective(s) in attending the course or conference. Describe your overall reaction to the course or conference and whether your expectation or objective(s) were met.

- Describe the course: state how it was presented and what you did.

- Mention what aspect of the course or conference was of particular value.

- Comment on the quality of the course or conference, covering

  the effectiveness of the presenters or instructors,

  the pacing (particularly for a course or seminar),

  the visual aids and handout materials, and

  the facilities.

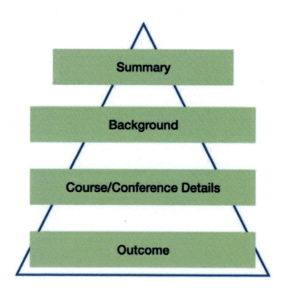

Figure 3-6: Writing Pyramid for course or conference attendance

Here is an example (continuing from the earlier scenario):

My objective was to increase my confidence when making oral presentations to clients and to in-house staff. I was also asked to evaluate the suitability of the seminar for other company employees. My objectives were fully met: practicing both planned and impromptu speaking has given me much greater confidence in preparing a presentation and responding to listeners' questions.

The seminar was divided into three sessions:
1. During the first two hours the seminar leader described informal and semiformal speaking techniques. She stressed the need for speakers to repeat an idea three times: start with an introductory summary, then provide the full detail, and end with a conclusion that sums up the main points.
2. The second half of the morning, the participants interviewed each other and presented a two-minute personal description. This was followed by impromptu two-minute presentations of a topic defined by the seminar leader.

3. The afternoon was devoted to practical speaking exercises, during which each participant presented a three-minute and a six-minute talk. I found this to be the most useful part of the seminar.

The seminar was very well presented. Ms. Porter-Farr established an informal setting that helped relax the participants. Yet she kept the seminar fast-paced and businesslike. There were 30 pages of handout notes that summarized the key points and provided exercises for future practice (see attached). The room at the Norfolk Hotel was a good size, but has acoustic problems: occasionally we could hear laughter and applause from the presentation in the next room.

4. In the Outcome or Action statement, sum up with an overall comment about the effectiveness of the course or conference and, if appropriate, include a recommendation:

The *Making Effective Oral Presentations* seminar provides a valuable learning experience. I recommend we either enroll staff to attend the next open-registration seminar (planned for January 27) or ask Ms. Porter-Farr to bring the seminar in-house. I've attached a cost sheet for both options.

Reporting an Inspection

People who are particularly good at their work sometimes are promoted to the position of inspector, so they can check on work done by others. In the building trades, for example, a skilled craftsperson may check on work being done at several small construction sites or act as the resident inspector on a large construction project.

These reports are called inspection reports, and are actually an extended field trip report. They follow the five-compartment writing pyramid shown in Figure 3-7.

1. The Summary Statement describes, in just a few words, the general condition you found or the overall impression you gained during your inspection. For example:

Installation of the data processing equipment is on schedule, but minor deficiencies may prevent switchover on the planned date.

2. The Background describes the circumstances relating to the inspection. Like a field trip report, it answers the question: *Who went where, why, and when?*

My visit to the Boris Lake site took place on September 13. Dave Jarvis authorized it in an email on September 8 and asked me to check on installation status.

3.   Under Conditions Found you describe what you observed during the inspection. If you are assessing the *quantity* of work done, these could be, for example, the

- *cubic metres* of concrete poured,

- *number* of doors hung, extent of painting completed,

- *depth* of excavation reached,

- *length* of cable installed, and

- *percentage* of piles sunk.

However, if you are assessing the *quality* of work done, you would comment on the condition of the work that has been done. For instance:

The wallpaper has been raggedly trimmed and had air bubbles under it.
Or
The *4Tell* software program has a bug that prevents the user from saving his or her work.

If you are commenting on both *quantity* and *quality*, you can broaden your descriptions like this:

Drape tracks have been installed in all rooms of the main floor, but the work has been poorly done. The track in room A3 is not properly centered, and the track in room A6 slopes downward from right to left.

Figure 3-7: Writing Pyramid for an inspection report

4. Deficiencies are all the things you feel must be corrected; the work that has not been done or has been poorly done. List each deficiency as a separate item, give it a number, and use strong, definite words to indicate that the work *must* be done or the item *must* be repaired. Use strong words such as *is to, will,* and *must*. Avoid weak words such as *should*. Here are two examples.

Weakly worded deficiencies:

1. The drape track over window 4 in room A6 should be realigned so that it appears horizontal.
2. The green and yellow wires to pin B of terminal 17 should be resoldered.

More strongly worded deficiencies:

1. The drape track over window 4 in room A6 must be realigned so that it appears horizontal.
2. The green and yellow wires to pin B of terminal 17 must be resoldered.

An even better and more affirmative way to list deficiencies is to put a strong verb at the start of each deficiency, such as *Replace, Reinstall, Insert,* or *Connect.* This turns your deficiency into a definite instruction:

1. **Realign the drape track over window 4 in room A6 so that it is horizontal.**
2. **Resolder the green and yellow wires to pin B of terminal 17.**

It's important to keep the conditions found and the deficiencies as two separate compartments within your report. If you state each deficiency immediately after describing the condition you observed, you will create a series of statements like this:

1. **On tower 5, in several places the space between cable lacings exceeds the maximum specified in directive EL283, para. 61. Additional lacing must be installed so the maximum spacing between lacings is no more than 0.90m.**

The result is a series of subparagraphs that are coherent in themselves, but in which a reader will have difficulty quickly identifying what corrective action needs to be taken. By keeping them as separate compartments, your readers will be able to find the deficiency easily and know that the list is complete.

An alternative way to list conditions and deficiencies is to create a table. The example in Figure 3-8 changes the title *Deficiency* to *Corrective Action.* This informs the reader specifically what has to be done.

Note that Conditions Found can be general statements, but Corrective Actions must state specifically what has to be done.

5. The Outcome/Action compartment has a dual purpose:

- To make a final comment about the site or project being inspected.
- To make a recommendation if further action needs to be taken.

For example:
Although the computer and integrated software have been properly installed, the system will not be fully operational until operator training is complete. The training will be finished by May 10. If an earlier start-up date is necessary, I recommend that two operators be flown to Toronto for training by Hazelton Systems Ltd.

Conditions Found	Corrective Action
1. Processor-controllers: 15 are operational, 2 are unserviceable.	1. Repair or replace processor controllers 4A and 7B.
2. Transmission by fibre optic cable to the remote site is satisfactory.	---------------------------
3. Two of the video monitors are Nabuchi model 100. The remainder are model 200.	3. Raise a requisition to replace older model 100 video monitors with new Nabuchi model 200.

Figure 3-8: An inspection report prepared as a table

Some employers use forms or templates for their inspector to write reports. This helps maintain consistency and considerably simplifies the inspectors' writing because it automatically divides the information into writing compartments.

Figure 3-9 shows the Background information is included in the first section. It is labelled Inspection Details and precedes the Summary Statement (called the Inspection Summary in this example).

Inspection Report

Inspection Details

Location: 521 Barclay Bay   Date: August 29

Items(s) Being Inspected: Interior Decoration

Inspector: Ray Dryfuss   Contractor: Phil-Dec Ltd.

Inspection Summary

Progress and workmanship are generally good, although some deficiencies need to be corrected.

Conditions Found

-The carpet for the living room and front hall has not been installed. The carpet has been received, but the underpad has not been delivered.

-All walls and ceiling have been painted and are satisfactory.

-All wallpaper has been hung. The work is satisfactory in the kitchen and bathroom, but not in the dining room.

-Trim around the doors and windows have been installed and is satisfactory.

-Tiles have been installed in the bathroom and kitchen and are satisfactory.

-The rubber baseboard has been poorly installed in the bathroom and kitchen.

Deficiencies

1. Install carpet and underpad in the living room and front hall.

2. Strip and rehang wallpaper in the dining room.

3. Clean up the mess around the baseboard in the kitchen and bathroom.

4. Install new baseboard where the previously installed baseboard does not fit properly.

Recommendations

1. Because of the delay in delivery of the under paid, I recommend that the invoice be paid (less $700) as soon as deficiencies 2 and 3 have been corrected.

Figure 3-9: An inspection report written using a template

Reporting Progress

When you are working on a project for an extended length of time, you will occasionally be asked to write a progress report for your supervisor or manager. Your report should answer three questions:

1. How is the job progressing?
2. Have you run into any problems and, if so, what have you done about them?
3. When will you complete the job and, if you are behind schedule, what action are you taking to try to finish on time?

The simplest way to present this information is in a logical sequence from the past, through the present, to the future. So, you have a five-compartment writing pyramid, as shown in Figure 3-10.

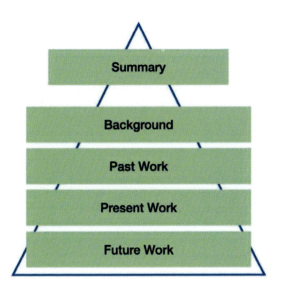

Figure 3-10: Writing Pyramid for a progress report

1. The Summary Statement is a particularly important feature of progress reports. Managers are especially interested in whether each project is on schedule and budget, so tell them right away what they most want to know. Here is an example, written by Candace to her project manager:

Although work at the construction site is two days behind schedule, I expect the crew to finish the job on May 18, the planned completion date.

Now that Candace has told her manager the project is behind schedule (but has immediately set the manger's mind at ease), she'll explain in the rest of the report how she arrived at this general statement.

2. In the Background compartment Candace describes factors affecting the job, such as project authorization details, contract number and date, who is involved in doing the work, and the project start and expected completion dates.
3. In the Past Work, Candance describes work she has done to date. If she had written a previous report, she can divide the Past Work into two segments:

    1. A general part, in which she describes what has been done since the job started.
    2. A more detailed part, in which she describes what has been done since the previous report was written.

The length and depth of topic coverage depends on the particular situation. If only a general statement of progress is necessary and the project has been running smoothly, then keep the Past Work entry short. For example:

Since arriving at the Port Coquitlam property on October 17, we have rebuilt the interiors of all six rooms and have painted two of them.

However, if the reader will want more exact information, or if there is a problem or unusual situation to report, then you will have to insert more details. These should include facts, such as the quantity of items completed, the number of hours worked, or the amount of material used. If there is an extensive list, attach it as a separate sheet and refer to it in the report.

4. In Present Work, Candace describes what is currently being done. This may be no more than a short paragraph or even a single sentence:

We are now cutting and installing indoor-outdoor carpet.

It can also describe what is being done to bring a delayed project back onto schedule:

The crew is working two hours overtime three evenings this week to recover 18 hours of lost time.

5. In Future Work, Candance tells the reader what she plans to do next and, if the project is behind schedule, forecasts a revised final completion date. If the job is running smoothly it can usually be a short statement:

The siding and shingles will be started on Monday so that, weather permitting, we will finish the job on Friday May 18.

But if there are problems and the project is behind schedule, Candance must tell her reader what her plans are and how she intends to put them into effect:

I plan to wire up the main control panel this week so the government inspector can check the building on May 13. I will then finish installing the control unit in room A301 and do the site operational test on May 16, two days behind schedule.

Figure 3-11 shows an example of a short progress report.

TO: Kelly Freeland

From: Glen Marguson

Date: August 15

Subject: Lunchroom Modernization Progress

Summary

At the midpoint of the lunchroom modernization project the contractor is roughly on schedule. We can expect to start using the lunchroom again on September 8, as planned.

Background

Past Work

During the first three weeks the contractor (Jorgensen Construction company of Guelph, Ontario) has completed all major construction work, installed new plumbing and wiring, and started the painting and decorating. He had to leave a space for the steam table, which will not be delivered until September 6, but says it can be installed in one day without disturbing other equipment. Currently he is building the lunch counter storage cabinets, buffet, and serving area.

Present Work

Future Work

The contractor estimates all construction, decorating, and major installation work will be completed by August 31. This will leave one week for the kitchen supplier to install and hook up the serving area equipment, which is scheduled to take only 2.5 days. The steam table will be installed and hooked up on September 7.

Figure 3-11: A short progress report

Reporting Project Completion

When you finish a project or task, you will be expected to write a report that documents key features about the work you did and whether any work is outstanding. In one sense, a project completion report is like a final progress report in that is has a five-compartment writing pyramid (see Figure 3-12).

Figure 3-12: Writing Pyramid for a project completion report

The writing compartments for a project completion report should contain the following information:
1. The Summary Statement identifies that the project is complete and states whether there is any special information the reader needs to know.
2. The Background is similar to that of a progress report: it states who authorized the project, its starting date and planned completion date, and who was involved.
3. The Project Highlights compartment describes the most important aspects of the project and what was achieved.
4. The Exceptions compartment identifies any variances from the original project plan and discusses why the variances were necessary, how they

affected the project, what actions were taken because of the variance, and whether any further action is necessary. For example:

At site 17, we were unable to install the AV61 sensor in the location specified by installation instruction SC28, para. 28.2. A humidity control box had already been installed in that location, so we constructed a 290 mm wide by 210 mm deep shelf to the left of the humidity control box and mounted the sensor on it. This called for additional cabling to connect the sensor to the master control station. A drawing of the installation is included in attachment 3.

5.   The final compartment is called either Outcome or Action:

- It is an Outcome if the project is complete and no further work needs to be done or no further decisions need to be made. In such cases the Outcome may be just a single sentence stating the project is complete.

- It is an Action if further work is necessary. The Action compartment lists what has to be done, and when and by whom it should be done. Here is an example:

I will arrange for a replacement standby power pack to be shipped to site 17, where I have left installation instructions with the resident technician. The power pack will be shipped on June 12 and installed by June 15.

Figure 3-13 shows a typical project completion report.

To: Janine Smyrna

From: Sandy Carstairs

Date: January 28

Subject: End-use of Model Nabuchi 280A tablets

Summary

My examination of customer purchase orders for the Nabuchi Model 280A tablets shows that we are entitled to a refund of $35,957.04 from Revenue Canada for duty paid on imported components.

Background

The 3000 model 280A tablets we manufactured between May 2018 and October 2019 each contained a circuit board that we bought from Nabuchi Industries in South Korea. We paid an import duty of $28.50 for each board. A November 15 ruling by Revenue Canada now permits imported components installed in products delivered to educational institutions to be brought into Canada duty-free. The ruling was subsequently made retroactive

Project Highlights

to January 1, which encompasses the entire run for the Model 280A. That is 21 months of production.

Our inventory shows that 2882 of the 3000 280A tablets we manufactured have been sold. My research into customer purchase orders and our invoices has identified 1259 units that were bought by educational institutions. This means we can claim a $28.56 refund on the 1259 units, for a total refund of $35,957.04

Exceptions

There were 84 units for which I was unable to identify an end use: 7 were purchased by customers who have since declared bankruptcy, 2 were destroyed in fires, 13 were stolen and not recovered, 34 were resold and therefore ineligible for a refund, and 28 could not be traced.

Outcome

I will prepare a claim to Revenue Canada for you to sign and, for the remaining 118 unsold units, I will keep a running record of purchases and declared end use.

Figure 3-13: A project completion report

Chapter 4

WRITING PROPOSALS

There are three types of proposals each with a different function:
- Short informal proposals

- Semiformal proposals

- Formal proposals

Short Informal Proposals

Informal proposals offer an idea and discuss how it should be implemented. Most informal proposals are written as internal communications between, for example, an employee and a supervisor within the same department, or between two people (usually supervisors or peers) in different departments. In each case the writer believes there is a better way to do something and proposes trying the new method. Typical informal proposals might be
- a suggestion from a staff member that the department buy a new graphics software package,

- a proposal to stagger break or lunchtimes, to avoid long lines at the cafeteria counter, or

- a request to attend a course or conference (a request is, in effect, a proposal).

Semiformal Proposals

Semiformal proposals can range from 1 or 2 pages to 30 or more pages. They may occasionally be written as an email but more often as a document and attached to an email. If the proposal is long or distributed to higher up executives, it may be preceded by a title page or have the heading PROPOSAL followed by a title centered at the top of the first page of text. In either case it is sent to the reader with a cover letter.

A semiformal proposal, may for example, suggest ways to increase productivity, improve a situation, resolve a problem, or conduct research. For example,

- a request from a production manager suggesting that the company research space for a new production line,

- a recommendation by a consultant proposing that a client reduce overhead costs by combining two departments,

- a proposal by a manager of field operations asking the company to supply tablets with cell connectivity to the construction crew supervisors, or

- a letter from a consultant specializing in the effects of high noise levels, proposing that the local airport authority measure sound levels under the approach path to the main runway where residents complain that aircraft flying overhead disturb their sleep.

Formal Proposals

Formal proposals are large and often multiple-volume documents designed to impress upon the client, often the government or a major organization, such as General Motors, that the proposing company has the capability to carry out an important, often multi-million-dollar task or project. They are substantial because they describe in detail what will be done, how it will be done, who will be responsible for specific aspects of the work, and why the proposing company has the potential to complete the project on time, within budget and to the client's satisfaction.

Formal proposals are normally prepared in response to a *Request for Proposal* (RFP) and are usually written as a team effort, operating under a tight delivery deadline. The RFP often defines exactly how the proposal is to be organized what topics must be covered and in what sequence, and, sometimes, how many pages are to be devoted to each topic. Typical examples would be

- a proposal to provide training services for a company with branches nationwide,

- a proposal to research ways of improving a bank's online services for customers, and

- a proposal to upgrade the communication systems for the military.

Because formal proposals are beyond the scope of this book, this chapter concentrates on preparing informal and semiformal proposals.

Impact on the Reader

The quality of a company's proposal often influences its acceptance. When Marie Havelock wanted to build a family room and a bathroom in her basement, she invited three renovation contractors to give her an estimate. They each visited her and she gave them a carefully drawn sketch of her ideas. Contractor A quoted a price over the phone, Contractor B texted her saying *"Our price for installing the family room and bathroom in your basement will be $5250.00 plus taxes."* Contractor C emailed her an attachment describing how the work would be done, how quickly the job would be completed, and what materials would be used. The document (proposal) included a detailed sketch and some recommendations for improving the plan Marie had provided. It also stated that the contractor would clean up and remove all construction debris from the site. The prices from all three contractors were similar.

Marie gave the job to contractor C because the detailed information in the attachment, plus its appearance, convinced her contractor C would be the most efficient and professional. Perhaps the other two contractors might have done a better job, but the *impression* they created seemed to indicate otherwise.

Proposal Design

The Pyramid Method™ applies to proposals, just as it does to reports. The number of compartments within the pyramid depends on the complexity of the proposal. All proposals, regardless of their length contain
1. a **Summary** that describes briefly what is being proposed and identifies any significant factors (such as cost),
2. the **Background** information that outlines why the proposal was prepared,
3. definitive **Details** that describe what needs to be done, how it will be done, what the results will be, and sometimes why the proposer has the capability to do the job (this is the body of the proposal),
4. an **Action Statement** that requests approval to go ahead or for the reader to make a decision or perform a specific action, and
5. **Appendices** that contain detailed evidence to support statements made in the body of the proposal.

Plan for an Informal Proposal

The writing plan for an informal proposal is shown in Figure 4-1. This is the form of proposal you will most often write when writing to people inside your organization or to people you have worked with before.

The five parts of the writing plan are described in more detail in Figure 4-2. The informal proposal shown in 4-3 was written to an internal audience and sent as an attachment to an email. The writing compartments can be readily identified, yet the writer did not feel that she had to adhere rigidly to them. This "comfortableness" makes the proposal easy to read.

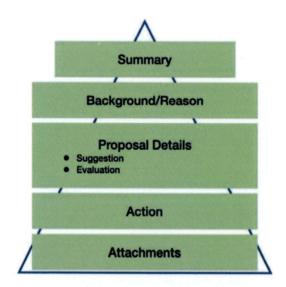

Figure 4-1: Writing plan for an informal proposal or suggestion

Compartment	Contents
Summary	What you want to do or want done (this is your main message)
Background	The circumstances that led up to your writing the proposal; the history.
Details	A detailed description of - the proposed change or improvements, why they are necessary, and what they will cost, and - an evaluation of the viability of the proposed changes and the effect they will have, including any problems that will evolve and how they will be overcome.
Action	A firm statement identifying what you want done, when, and by whom.
Attachments	Supporting data such as drawings, plans, cost estimates, and statistics.

Figure 4-2: The parts of an informal proposal

To: Vince Warchuk, Production Manager

From: Tara Williamson, Supervisor PC Lab

Subject: PC Lab Equipment Purchase

Date: June 23

Summary

I propose purchasing a Nabuchi 2100 video conferencing system for installation in the PC Lab and buying an annual subscription for the 4Tell cloud delivery platform which will include training and support for 12 months. The cost will be $15,990.

Background

The interactive virtual training for our team will be scheduled 4 weeks after the equipment has been installed. However, over the next two years, we will still need to provide training on a continuing basis for about 24 employees who will be responsible for maintaining upgrades and for facilitating others using the system. Access to the online training library will be $145 per person which calculates to a $3480 training expense, which is not included in my costs.

Details

I have evaluated the initial 60-minute webinar in the library and it is not only delivered professionally, but also it is very interactive, engaging, and educational. It is divided into short 5-minute modules which makes it easy to start and stop. I also had an employee who is not experienced with the 4Tell platform evaluate it and he gave it a positive review.

I plan to position the video conferencing equipment beside the computer console next to station 21, the last station in row 2 in the lab. To help with the audio and to ease the noise levels, I have included four headsets with microphones in my estimate. Specific purchase details are listed on the attachment. Here is a cost breakdown:

1. Nabuchi 2100 conferencing system	$10850
2. Four Headsets: TSR model 40	950
3. Cable junction box	240
4. 4Tell licensing (12 months)	3950
Total:	$15,990

Action

May I have your approval to use $15,990 from the capital equipment budget to purchase the video conferencing system and accompanying equipment?

Tara

Figure 4-3 An informal proposal prepared for an internal reader

Plan for a Basic Semiformal Proposal

The writing plan for a semiformal proposal is similar to that for an informal proposal, but the **Details** compartment is expanded to have two more subcompartments, as shown in Figure 4-4. There also is an additional compartment, known as the **Attachments** or **Appendices**, which holds data that supports statements made in the body of the proposal. Generally, Attachments (numbered 1, 2, 3) are used for semiformal proposals and Appendices (labelled A, B, C) are used for formal proposals. Figure 4-5 describes in more detail what is included in each part of the writing plan.

The semiformal proposal in Figure 4-6 was written by Mavis Hamilton of Floral West Imports. When writing the proposal, Mavis adopted the pyramid writing plan illustrated in Figure 4-4 and described in Figure 4-5, making some adaptations to suit her particular situation. The following numbered comments correspond to the numbers beside the figure.

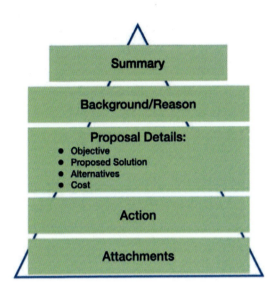

Figure 4-4: The writing plan for a semiformal proposal

Compartment	Contents
Summary	A synopsis of the key points of your proposal. It should identify the purpose, main advantages, result(s), and the cost(s). This information is drawn from the Background, Details, and Action compartments. In more formal proposals, the Summary may be called the Abstract.
Background/ Reason	A description of the situation, condition, or problem that demands attention and the circumstances leading up to it. This part is often called the Introduction.

Proposal Details	An introductory statement followed by four subcompartments:

- The **Objective** defines what needs to be achieved to improve the situation or condition, or to resolve the problem, and establishes the criteria that must be met. The objective may also be positioned at the end of the **Introduction**.
- The **Proposed Solution** offers what the writer considers to be the best way to achieve the objective. It includes a full description of the solution, the expected result or improvement, how the solution will be implemented, its advantages and disadvantages, and its cost.
- The **Alternatives** compartment describes alternatives to the proposed solution.
- The **Cost** identifies the total cost and sometimes secondary costs, depending on whether there are alternatives the reader may adopt. Often only the total cost is shown here and a breakdown of costs is placed in the Attachments.

Action	A recommendation of what action needs to be taken. It is often called **Recommendations** and needs to be written in strong, confident terms.
Attachments	Any documents or figures that support or explain the statements made in the body of the proposal, for example, drawings, sketches, cost analyses and spreadsheets.

Figure 4-5: The parts of a semiformal proposal

Floral West Imports Ltd.

470 Langley Avenue
PO Box 87061 North Vancouver Postal Station
North Vancouver BC V7L 4L6

**Proposal for Supplying Tropical Plants
to Pacific Restaurants Limited**

Prepared for

**Mr. David Wing Lee,
General Operations Manager
Pacific Restaurants Limited**

(1) We are proposing to supply Pacific Restaurants Limited with tropical plants for its "tropical rain forest" theme restaurants, and North American plants for its "Pacific Nook" restaurants. The plants in the rain forest restaurants will be rotated every two weeks to achieve a lush, constantly changing scene. Those in the Pacific Nook restaurants will remain, but will be trimmed and watered regularly and replaced before any signs of wilting occur. The cost for providing this service will be either

(2) $1305 or $1365 per month, depending on the level of service.

(3) **Introduction**   In a letter dated August 24, 2000, and at a subsequent meeting on September 4, Mr. David Wing Lee, General Operations Manager of Pacific Restaurants Limited, asked Floral West Imports for a proposal to supply and maintain plants in its 20 Greater Vancouver area restaurants. The contract would last for 12 months starting October 2000.

(4) There are two types of restaurants. The four "tropical rain forest" theme restaurants comprise

- *The Rain Forest* on Denman Street, Vancouver,
- *The Occasional Shower* on West Broadway, Vancouver,
- *The Samoan Retreat* in New Westminster, and
- *The Barbary Coast* in Horseshoe Bay.

These restaurants are to be filled entirely with lush tropical plants.

The sixteen smaller restaurants, called *Pacific Nooks*, have various locations in Vancouver, Burnaby, and West Vancouver. They are to have a selection of North American plants.

1

Figure 4-6: A semiformal business proposal

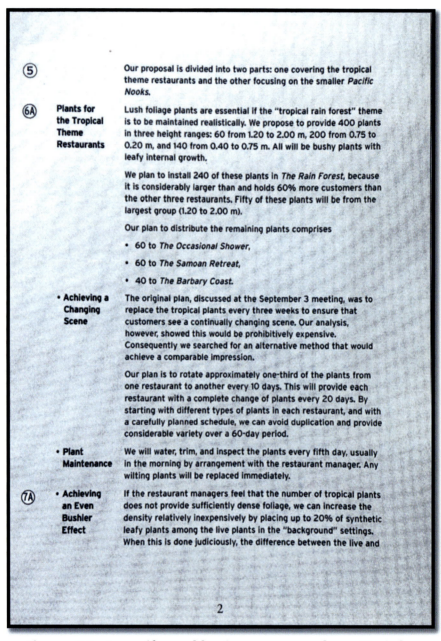

⑤ Our proposal is divided into two parts: one covering the tropical theme restaurants and the other focusing on the smaller *Pacific Nooks*.

⑥Ⓐ **Plants for the Tropical Theme Restaurants** Lush foliage plants are essential if the "tropical rain forest" theme is to be maintained realistically. We propose to provide 400 plants in three height ranges: 60 from 1.20 to 2.00 m, 200 from 0.75 to 0.20 m, and 140 from 0.40 to 0.75 m. All will be bushy plants with leafy internal growth.

We plan to install 240 of these plants in *The Rain Forest*, because it is considerably larger than and holds 60% more customers than the other three restaurants. Fifty of these plants will be from the largest group (1.20 to 2.00 m).

Our plan to distribute the remaining plants comprises

- 60 to *The Occasional Shower*,

- 60 to *The Samoan Retreat*,

- 40 to *The Barbary Coast*.

• **Achieving a Changing Scene** The original plan, discussed at the September 3 meeting, was to replace the tropical plants every three weeks to ensure that customers see a continually changing scene. Our analysis, however, showed this would be prohibitively expensive. Consequently we searched for an alternative method that would achieve a comparable impression.

Our plan is to rotate approximately one-third of the plants from one restaurant to another every 10 days. This will provide each restaurant with a complete change of plants every 20 days. By starting with different types of plants in each restaurant, and with a carefully planned schedule, we can avoid duplication and provide considerable variety over a 60-day period.

• **Plant Maintenance** We will water, trim, and inspect the plants every fifth day, usually in the morning by arrangement with the restaurant manager. Any wilting plants will be replaced immediately.

⑦Ⓐ • **Achieving an Even Bushier Effect** If the restaurant managers feel that the number of tropical plants does not provide sufficiently dense foliage, we can increase the density relatively inexpensively by placing up to 20% of synthetic leafy plants among the live plants in the "background" settings. When this is done judiciously, the difference between the live and

2

Figure 4-6: A semiformal business proposal, continued

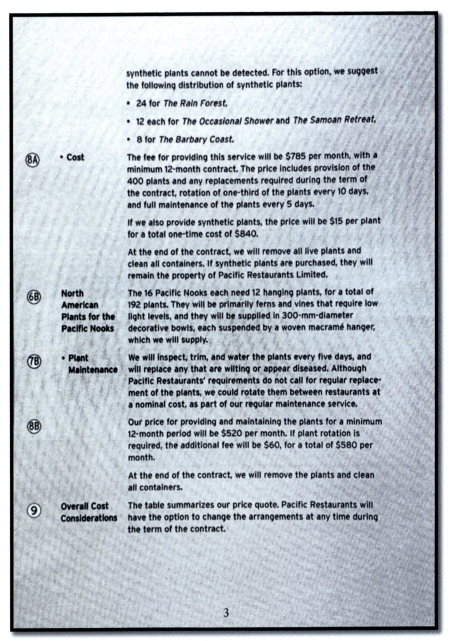

synthetic plants cannot be detected. For this option, we suggest the following distribution of synthetic plants:

- 24 for *The Rain Forest*,
- 12 each for *The Occasional Shower* and *The Samoan Retreat*,
- 8 for *The Barbary Coast*.

(8A) • Cost — The fee for providing this service will be $785 per month, with a minimum 12-month contract. The price includes provision of the 400 plants and any replacements required during the term of the contract, rotation of one-third of the plants every 10 days, and full maintenance of the plants every 5 days.

If we also provide synthetic plants, the price will be $15 per plant for a total one-time cost of $840.

At the end of the contract, we will remove all live plants and clean all containers. If synthetic plants are purchased, they will remain the property of Pacific Restaurants Limited.

(6B) North American Plants for the Pacific Nooks — The 16 Pacific Nooks each need 12 hanging plants, for a total of 192 plants. They will be primarily ferns and vines that require low light levels, and they will be supplied in 300-mm-diameter decorative bowls, each suspended by a woven macramé hanger, which we will supply.

(7B) • Plant Maintenance — We will inspect, trim, and water the plants every five days, and will replace any that are wilting or appear diseased. Although Pacific Restaurants' requirements do not call for regular replacement of the plants, we could rotate them between restaurants at a nominal cost, as part of our regular maintenance service.

(8B) Our price for providing and maintaining the plants for a minimum 12-month period will be $520 per month. If plant rotation is required, the additional fee will be $60, for a total of $580 per month.

At the end of the contract, we will remove the plants and clean all containers.

(9) Overall Cost Considerations — The table summarizes our price quote. Pacific Restaurants will have the option to change the arrangements at any time during the term of the contract.

3

Figure 4-6: A semiformal business proposal, continued

Service	Cost per month	One-time Cost
Supply, maintain, and rotate plants in 4 tropical theme restaurants	$785	
Supply and maintain plants in 16 *Pacific Nooks*	$520	
Subtotal	**$1305**	
Optional service: Install synthetic plants in theme restaurants		$840
Optional service: Rotate plants between *Pacific Nook* restaurants	$60	
Total	**$1365**	**$840**

If Pacific Restaurants chooses to extend the contract into subsequent years, the cost will be 20% less for year two, and 25% less for year three.

⑩ **To Sum Up**   Our proposal will provide a lush setting for Pacific Restaurants' tropical theme restaurants, and a fresh, pleasant appearance for the company's *Pacific Nook* restaurants. I will gladly provide more information and answer any questions concerning our proposal.

⑪ *Mavis J. Hamilton*

Mavis J. Hamilton
President

Floral West Imports Ltd.
September 7, 2000

4

Figure 4-6: A semiformal business proposal, continued

1. This paragraph is Mavis's **Summary**. She identifies the key features of her proposal and indents the paragraph from both margins to draw the reader's eye to it.

2. Not everyone likes to put the total cost up front. Some people fear that, if the cost seems high, the reader may not read the remainder of the proposal. Mavis counters this by saying: "The cost is what readers most want to know! They are going to search for it anyway so I might as well place it where they can find it."

3. The four paragraphs of the Introduction form Mavis's **Background** compartment. She starts by establishing her terms of reference (i.e. the purpose for writing the proposal).

4. In this and the next paragraph she describes the restaurants to demonstrate to her reader (who know all of this) that *she* fully understands what has to be done.

5. In this single sentence Mavis describes her **Approach** and, simultaneously, the scope of the proposal. (The three compartments, *Purpose, Situation,* and *Scope,* should be present in the Introduction to all longer reports and proposals.) In her Approach she is also telling her reader that *the Proposed Solution, Alternatives,* and *Cost* will be described twice: once for each type of restaurant.

6. In the section shown with 6A, Mavis describes specifically what she will do to provide the service desired for the first set of restaurants. In 6B she describes the service she will provide for the second set of restaurants.

7. In section 7A and 7B she describes alternatives the reader may choose to adopt.

8. In 8A she provides two costs for the first type of restaurant: one for the Proposed Solution and one covering the Alternatives. In 8B she provides the cost for the second type of restaurant.

9. Because there are several options, Mavis summarizes them in a table to help the reader quickly grasp the breakdown of Alternatives and their Cost.

10. As the table has already provided a terminal summary, she concludes with an **Outcome** rather than an Action Statement. In such cases, an Action Statement would be more likely to appear in the cover letter accompanying the proposal.

11. Mavis's proposal is a good illustration of how to use Information Design to create an effective proposal.

Plan for a Comprehensive Semiformal Proposal

A comprehensive semiformal proposal differs from the previous semiformal proposal in several ways:

- It usually deals with a more complex situation, such as a problem or an unsatisfactory condition, for which it proposes a solution or resolution.

- It discusses the circumstances in more detail.

- It establishes definitive criteria for the proposed changes.

- It frequently offers alternatives rather than just a single suggestion.

- It analyzes the proposed alternative in depth.

- It has a more formal appearance.

The writing compartments for a comprehensive semiformal proposal are shown in Figure 4-7. They contain the following information:

1. The **Summary** briefly describes the main highlights of the proposal, mostly drawn from the **Background, Proposal Details,** and **Outcome/Action** compartments. If headings are used in the proposal, this compartment is titled *Summary* or *Abstract*.

2. The **Background** compartment introduces the problem, situation, or unsatisfactory condition, and outlines the circumstances leading up to it. It is usually titled Introduction.

3. The **Proposal Details** start with the **Objective**, which defines what needs to be achieved to resolve the problem and establishes **Criteria** for an ideal solution. This information may be included as part of the *Introduction* or preceded by a heading of its own, such as *Requirements* or *Criteria*.

4. **The Plan** describes, in-depth, how the problem can be resolved or the situation improved. It comprises

- a description of the solution,

- the result or improvement it will achieve,

- how it will be implemented,

- its advantages and disadvantages, and

- its cost.

5. If there are **Alternatives**, they are arranged in descending order of suitability. This and the previous compartment may be preceded by a single heading, such as *Methods for Increasing Productivity*, or by several descriptive headings, one for each alternative.

6. The **Evaluation** compartment analyzes and compares the alternative solutions, with particular reference to the criteria established in the **Objective**. It may briefly discuss the effects of

- adopting the proposed solution,

- adopting each of the alternative solutions, and

- adopting none of the solutions (i.e. taking no action).

7. The **Outcome** should be divided into two compartments:

- **Conclusions**, which summarize the key result(s).

- **Recommendation**s, which state clearly what action should be taken. Recommendations should be worded in strong, positive terms and should be titled *Recommendation(s)*

8. The **Evidence** compartment, if used, contains detailed analyses, test results, drawings, etc. that support and amplify statements made in the previous compartments. It usually is titled *Attachments* or *Appendices*.

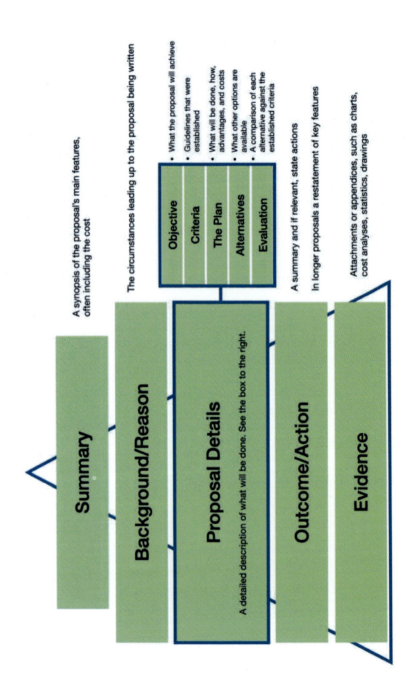

Figure 4-7: Writing plan for a comprehensive semiformal proposal

Plan for a Formal Proposal

Formal proposals are normally lengthy documents, which sometimes run to
several volumes. Most formal proposals are written in response to a Request for
Proposal (RFP) issued by the government or a large commercial organization.
Often the RFP stipulates the major topics each proposing company must
address, the sequence in which the information must be presented and
sometimes, the maximum number of words for each section. Although there is
some similarity between the format stipulated by the different agencies issuing
RFPs, there are sufficient variations to make it impossible to present a
"standard" outline here. The sections listed below are a composite of several
outlines.

The major compartments of a formal proposal are illustrated in Figure 4-8.
When the compartments are converted to headings, the outline looks like this:

> Letter of Transmittal (optional)
> Cover
> Title Page
> Summary
> Table of Contents
> Introduction
> The Problem (Description of the Problem or Situation)
> The Approach (Approach to Resolving the Problem or Situation)
> Organization and Planning
> Exceptions
> Price Proposal
> Experience
> > -Company
> > -Employees
> Evidence (Appendices)

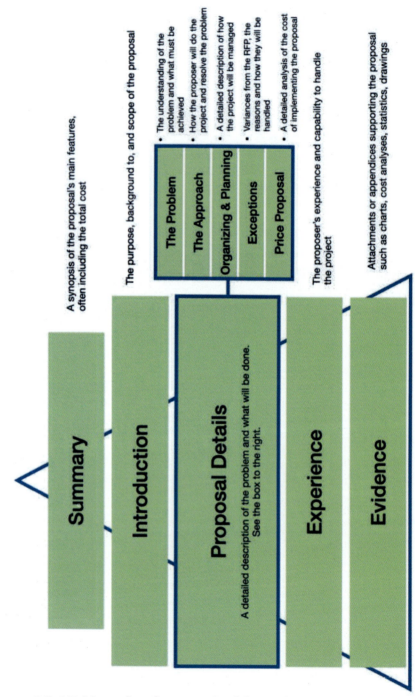

A synopsis of the proposal's main features, often including the total cost

The purpose, background to, and scope of the proposal

- The understanding of the problem and what must be achieved
- How the proposer will do the project and resolve the problem
- A detailed description of how the project will be managed
- Variances from the RFP, the reasons and how they will be handled
- A detailed analysis of the cost of implementing the proposal

The Problem

The Approach

Organizing & Planning

Exceptions

Price Proposal

The proposer's experience and capability to handle the project

Attachments or appendices supporting the proposal such as charts, cost analyses, statistics, drawings

Summary

Introduction

Proposal Details

A detailed description of the problem and what will be done. See the box to the right.

Experience

Evidence

Figure 4-8: Writing plan for a typical formal proposal

Letter of Transmittal

When attached to a formal proposal, a letter of transmittal assumes much greater importance than the standard cover letter attached to the front of a semiformal or formal report. Normally signed by an executive of the proposing company, it comments on the most significant aspects of the proposal and sometimes the cost. It is similar to the Executive Summary for a long report.

Summary

The Summary mentions the purpose of the proposal, touches briefly on its highlights, and states the total cost. If an Executive Summary is bound inside the proposal, the Summary is often omitted.

Introduction

As in a report, the Introduction describes the background, purpose, and scope of the proposal. If the proposal is prepared in response to an RFP, it refers to the RFP and the specific terms of reference or requirements stipulated by the originating authority.

Description of Problem or Situation

This section describes the problem that needs to be resolved or the situation that needs to be improved. It usually includes
- a statement of the problem or situation, as defined by the RFP,

- an elaboration of the problem or situation and its implications (to demonstrate the proposer's full understanding of the circumstances), and

- the proposers understanding of any constraints or special requirements.

Approach to Resolving Problem or Improving Situation

The proposer describes how the company will tackle the problem or situation and states specifically *what* will be done, *why* it will be done, and, in broad terms, *how* it will be done. As this is the proposer's solution to the problem or method for resolving the situation, this section must be written in strong, definite, convincing terms, which will give the reader confidence that the proposing company knows how to undertake the task.

Organization and Planning

Here, the *how* of the Approach section is expanded to show exactly what steps the proposer will take.

- Under **Organization**, the proposer describes how a project group will be established, its composition, its relationship to other components of the proposing company, and how it will interface with the client's organization.

- Under **Planning**, the proposer outlines a complete project plan and, for each stage or aspect, exactly what steps will be taken and what will be achieved or accomplished.

Exceptions

Sometimes a company may conceive an unusual approach that not only solves the problem but also offers significant advantages, yet deviates from one or more of the client's specified requirements. These exceptions are listed and the reason why each need not be met is clearly explained.

Price Proposal

The proposer's price for the project is stated as an overall price and then broken down into schedules for each phase of the project. The extent and method of pricing is usually specified by the RFP.

This section of the proposal may be placed in various positions. The RFP may stipulate that it appear at the front, as an attachment, or as a separate document.

Experience

The proposing company describes its overall experience and history and its particular experience in resolving problems or handling situations similar to those described in the RFP. It details the key persons who will be assigned to the project and describes their experience in a curriculum vitae (CV) or resume.

Appendices

The appendices contain supporting documents, specifications, large drawings and flow charts, schedules, equipment lists, etc – all of which are referenced in the proposal.

Chapter 5

CUSTOMIZING YOUR DOCUMENTS

So far we've talked about how to organize and structure your information into logical and easy-to-understand documents. In this chapter we are going to suggest additional ways for you to write and present your information so it is appealing to read, easy to find, and adaptable to other cultures. You have only one chance, in writing, to make your best impression.

Designing Your Information to Draw Attention

You can help your readers understand and access information through the appearance of your documents. We call this **Information Design.** The suggestions we provide here will help your information "jump off the page" and make it easier to read and understand. The content and structure of your document is still important, but using Information Design techniques will enhance its readability.

Insert Headings

In longer documents, particularly those addressing several aspects of a situation, you can help your reader find information by using headings. Headings serve as an outline of or road map to your content. Each heading must be informative, summarizing clearly what is covered in the paragraphs that follow. If, for instance, we had replaced the heading preceding this paragraph with the single word "Headings" it would not have been as descriptive.

NEVER USE ALL CAPTIAL LETTERS FOR A HEADING, BECAUSE IT MAKES THE WORDS MORE DIFFICULT TO READ.

Studies show that only 23% of readers actually read titles set in all capital letters. Similarly, underling also makes the text more difficult to read. Underlines were used when documents were typed on typewriters and writers did not have the options today's software provide. There is no reason to use an underline when there are so many other ways to emphasize text. The structure of your headings must, however, be consistent throughout the text. For example, you can use different sizes of the *same* font, set in bold and/or italicized letters:

Level 1 heading (14 point bold) **Form Strong Sentences**

Level 2 heading (12 point bold) Write Emphatic Sentences

Level 3 heading (12 point bold/italic) *Use the Active Voice*

Here are some suggestions for integrating headings into the text.

Centre Main Headings

A main heading should be centered in the middle of the page. This is reserved for major topics, like "Introduction". Set them in a larger boldface type so they stand out from the rest of the text.

Centre Subsidiary Headings

A subsidiary heading is also positioned in the middle of the page, but does not have the same emphasis as the main heading. Sometimes a subsidiary heading is used as a subtitle to a main heading. Set subsidiary headings in boldface type and in a type that is smaller than the Main Heading, but larger than the body text.

Side Headings

Side headings introduce a new section of text, are usually set in boldface or italics or in a larger type size than the body text to show emphasis, and are set flush with the left margin. Paragraphs following a side heading are also set with all lines flush with the left margin. In contemporary writing, the first line of each paragraph is seldom indented.

Subparagraph Headings and Subparagraphing

Subparagraph headings and the text that follows them are indented about five spaces or to a 1 cm tab position. The first line is not indented further. Each subparagraph is typed as a solid block, which helps readers see the subordination of ideas. Indenting the entire paragraph is another way of visually helping the reader.

Headings Built Into a Paragraph: Continue the text immediately after the heading, on the same line. Paragraph headings like these can be used for main paragraphs, subparagraphs, and secondary subparagraphs. Usually, a paragraph heading applies only to one paragraph of text. The headings can be italic, bold, or both, but never underlined.

Subparagraphing Combined with Paragraph Numbering

If you are numbering your paragraphs and need to integrate headings into the text, as can happen with a long document, manual, or procedure, similar rules apply:

1. Side Headings
    1.1. When paragraph numbers are used, side headings normally are assigned simple consecutive numbers as has been done here.
    1.2. Where only one paragraph follows a side heading, it is not assigned a separate paragraph number and is typed with its left margin flush with the side heading, as has been done in the paragraph immediately below heading 1.3.
    1.3. Subparagraph Headings and Subparagraphing
    If more than one paragraph follows a subparagraph heading, each is assigned an identifiable number or letter:
    1.3.1 This would be the first subparagraph.
    1.3.2 This would be the second subparagraph.
    1.3.3 Each subparagraph can be further subdivided into a series of very short secondary subparagraphs:
    1.3.3.1 Here is a secondary subparagraph.
    1.3.3.2 Ideally each secondary subparagraph should contain no more than one sentence.
    1.3.4 *Inserting a Heading:* Secondary subparagraphs may also be assigned subparagraph headings.

Choose Only One Font

A font, such as Century Schoolbook or Arial, is a set of characters with the same features. Fonts are divided into *serif* (they have a slight finishing stroke: T) and **sans serif** (they don't have a finishing stroke: T). The font you choose will project an image of you, your company, and your document:

- Statistics show that serif fonts, like Century Schoolbook and Times New Roman, are easier to read on paper because the finishing stroke of each letter leads the reader's eye to the next letter. Consequently, serif fonts should be used for longer documents. For example, this text is printed in Iowan Old Style.

- Sans serif fonts, like Arial, or Helvetica, are clean, clear, and portray a neat and modern image, yet are not as easy to read on paper and are only suitable for shorter paper documents. However, sans serif fonts are easier to read online (email or website) or in a slide presentation (PowerPoint).

Once you decide on a font you should stay with it. Don't use a different font to show emphasis. Rather use **boldface,** *italics,* or a larger point size to emphasize your text. Logos and sometimes headings are excluded from this guideline.

Make sure that the character size you choose is appropriate for your document and audience. In a one-page letter you may use a 10 point size to help keep the content to one page. In a longer document, use a 12 point size: the type will be slightly larger and the reader's eyes won't tire as easily as with a smaller point size.

Justify Only on the Left

Our software makes it easy to justify both the left and right margins, which means all lines begin and end at exactly the same place on both sides of the page. The software auto adjusts the spaces between words and characters to force the right margin to be straight. These spaces will make the words either too crowded or too far apart, which strains the reader's eyes because they constantly have to adjust to the uneven spacing. It may seem like only a subtle difference, yet it's something you can control to make reading more comfortable.

We recommend you justify only the text on the left and leave the right side "ragged"

Use Margins to Draw Attention

Many people hesitate to change the standard settings that come with their software packages. Yet once they see the value of being unique, they are easily convinced to try a new way. Try using a left-hand column for headings (about 1/3 of the page), and a right-hand column for the text. This helps draw reader's eyes and attention to the headings so they can skim and retrieve information quicker.

Figure 5-1 shows two proposals. One (a) is presented in the traditional format with the text justified to the left margin, while the other, (b), is presented with a left-hand margin for headings and a right-hand margin for text. The latter takes up more space, but makes the information much more accessible. See Mavis Hamilton's proposal in the previous chapter for an example (Figure 4-6).

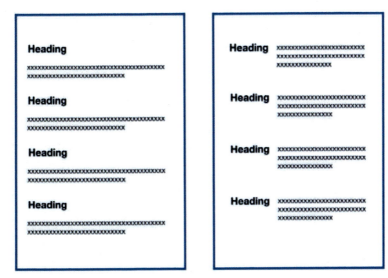

Figure 5-1: Two different ways to present headings

Use White Space to Break Up Text

Adding white space or areas without text is another valuable Information Design technique. You can also use diagrams and figures to break up long passages of text and to complement the message. A simple flow chart or table makes a nice diversion for the reader and presents the information in a more visual and concrete way.

Pictures help explain concepts and aid the visual learner. For example, if you write an incident report describing an accident in which you were involved, you could spend paragraphs describing in detail the position of the vehicle prior to, during, and after the accident. Or you could sketch a neat diagram and insert or attach it to the document.

Use Lists to Break Up Information

The appearance of your paragraphs may make your readers less receptive to your information. Lists or subparagraphs can help break up text and make it visually more attractive. Here is an excerpt from a report written without Information Design concepts:

Opening a service office in Red Deer, Alberta will help us to be more responsive as a service provider to the Red Deer business community. We will be able to meet customers' requests for service much more quickly. On average, response time will be cut by 1.5 hours compared to the current travel time from either our Calgary or Edmonton offices. In addition, we will reduce travel costs. Because service time is charged at a standard hourly rate, we currently bear all travel costs. Having service representatives come from a local office will reduce these travel costs to an almost negligible amount. Third, we will be able to increase our company's visibility to the Red Deer business community. Sales representatives report they currently have difficulty convincing potential clients that we can respond rapidly to urgent demands for service. A *local* service office will put an end to this fear.

A reader facing a long paragraph of text like this will subconsciously expect it to be "heavy going" and will start reading it unenthusiastically, with possibly a negative attitude to your information. This makes it much harder for you, as a writer, to encourage your readers to accept your ideas. You can avoid this resistance if you break the information into smaller chunks and form a list.

If we break up the second sentence and add a bulleted or numbered list of the suggestions, the information is more attractive and easier to read and understand.

Opening a service office in Red Deer, Alberta will help us to be more responsive as a service provider to the Red Deer business community. We will experience three main benefits:

1. **Meet customers' requests for service much more quickly. On average, response time will be cut by 1.5 hours compared to the current travel time from either our Calgary or Edmonton offices.**

2. **Reduce travel costs. Because service time is charged at a standard hourly rate, we currently bear all travel costs. Having service representatives come from a local office will reduce these travel costs to an almost negligible amount.**

3. **Increase our company's visibility to the Red Deer business community. Sales representatives report they currently have difficulty convincing potential clients that we can respond rapidly to urgent demands for service. A *local* service office will put an end to this fear.**

These three subparagraphs contain the same information as the initial non-stop paragraph but the information does not seem so overwhelming. In fact, readers know, before they read a word, that they are going to be presented with three ideas.

Use Tables for Text

Using tables to display information can also help you design your information for maximum impact. Many people reserve tables for numerical data; we suggest using them to present text in an easily accessible format to compartmentalize the information. Figure 5-2 shows a table designed to describe the writing compartments for a request.

Writing Plan for a Request	
Compartment	Contents
Summary	A brief description of your request
Background or Reason	The circumstances leading up to the request
Request Details	A detailed explanation of what your request includes, what will be gained if the request is approved, any problems the request may cuase, and what the cost will be
Action	A statement that identifies clearly what you ant the reader to do after reading your request

Figure 5-2: Using a table to present text

Use Columns to Increase Readability

Although columns are not suitable for simple daily emails and documents, they certainly can be used for reports or proposals. The value of using columns is described in Figure 5-3

Setting Text in Two Columns Increases Readability

Using a magazine-style, two-column printed text area helps guide the reader. The line length is forced to be shorter so a reader's eye can follow the line easily and therefore is less stressed. Imagine how difficult it would be to read a magazine that was printed in one long six-inch-wide column!

We don't recommend this format for letters or short reports but it can have a good impact on longer reports and technical proposals.

This column format is especially useful when you insert graphics into a document. Text and graphics can be clearly integrated by "wrapping" text around the image. The two are then visually linked.

Graphics that are used in a two-column format also help to balance the page. Often a graphic is inserted and seems to be isolated because there is too much white space around it. With two columns, one column offsets the other.

Another benefit of the two-column format is that it forces the writer to use shorter paragraphs; otherwise, the column would be a big block of text without any breaks.

Figure 5-3: The benefits of setting text in columns

Writing for an International Audience

In our global economy, we must pay even more attention to identifying who we are writing to, and to tailor the message to that person. Often this means learning a different set of rules for communicating with new customers and business associates.

You need to be sensitive to the idea that in many cultures starting with a Summary Statement (getting right down to business) may be considered rude.

Writing Business Correspondence

Often, business people (especially North Americans) try explaining that they start with the most important information right away because it's more efficient to put the main message up front. However, we must remember other cultures have their own centuries-old traditions of communication, and recognize that *we* have to adapt our own methods of communication to suit them. As our world becomes smaller with global communications, writers must understand the culture prevalent in each society they write to and make adjustments in their writing so they do not offend their readers.

In adjusting your writing, though, you do not need to entirely discard the Pyramid Method™. You can still use the pyramid for the central part of your message, but you need to precede it with a personal greeting and polite remarks concerning the health and happiness of your reader and, often, of your reader's family. You will also need to end your message with a polite closing remark, such as wishing the reader continuing good health and prosperity in the months and years ahead. Figure 5-4 shows how to adapt the pyramid for readers beyond the Western cultures.

Figure 5-4: Adapted Pyramid for non-Western readers

This adaptation is appropriate for readers you have previously corresponded with. However, to new or more traditional readers, placing the Summary Statement so close to the greeting may still seem too abrupt. For these audiences, move the Summary Statement further down in the correspondence. The revised writing pyramid looks like this:

1. Greeting
2. Background
3. Details
4. Outcome and Summary Statement (combined)
5. Complimentary Close

These revised writing pyramids apply to all formal business letters and email.

Some Writing Guidelines

Changing the order of information is not the only part of a message that requires attention. When you write to readers whose English is a second language, you need to choose words that will be clearly understood. This also is true for some English speaking cultures. In the United Kingdom, for instance, the word "fortnight" meaning "two weeks" is commonly used, yet in the United States and even in parts of Canada, it might not be understood. Similarly, the word "presently" has a different meaning in the US and the UK. Here are some guidelines:

- Avoid long, complex words. If you have a choice between two or more words or expressions that have roughly the same meaning, choose the simpler of the two. For example, write "pay" rather than "salary" or "remuneration."

- Use the same word to describe the same action or product consistently throughout your document. Decide, for example, whether you will refer to money in the bank as *funds, currency, deposits, or money*. We often use the word "capital" to refer to money, yet we should avoid it when writing to international audiences since it may be misinterpreted as a reference to a city (capitol).

- Always use a word in the same sense. You could confuse an English as a second language (ESL) reader if you were to write in one sentence, *"It would not be appropriate to transfer funds from Account A to Account B"* (meaning it would not be suitable to do so), and then in another, *"We had insufficient funds to appropriate Company A"* (meaning to take over or buy out Company A).

Meeting and Speaking

When visiting other countries, it's important you understand and adapt to their local culture and business etiquette. People in Eastern Europe for instance, have major but subtle differences between western and eastern perceptions of good manners and effective communication techniques. For example, it is inappropriate to start meeting by immediately describing why everyone is there and what you want to accomplish.

At the start of a meeting between North American and Russian business people, members of both companies would sit around a table, be served refreshments, be introduced to each other, and engage in polite conversation about travel, where they live, the weather, and the health of each other's families. Business should *never* be brought up at the start of the meeting. It is also bad manners to pour yourself a second cup of coffee: that is *always* the host's prerogative, because the action would imply that your host has not been hospitable enough. Nothing would be said, but the sudden pause in conversation would tell you that you'd committed a faux pas.

The business discussion starts when the topic is eventually introduced by a member of the host country. Only then should you start describing your plans and ideas, and even then you'll discover it should be done in a roundabout way. Where we are accustomed to putting the main message right up front, using the *tell-tell-tell* method of presenting information, in some countries, it is more customary to start with a brief history of the subject and then lead into the point you want to make. Remember, too, to choose your words carefully, because your hosts may not interpret some words in the same way we do.

Some Cultural Differences

In some cultures, for example, if you were told *"It really would not be convenient to pay your hotel expenses by credit card"* you might assume that it could be done but that it is the *less-preferred* method when, in fact, *"It would not be convenient"* is really a polite way of saying that it simply *cannot* be done (perhaps because they don't have the facilities for accepting credit cards).

Similarly, in some Pacific Rim countries it is severely impolite to directly contradict a speaker or to say "No" to a suggestion. You should nod your head and say something like:" That is a possibility" or "We will consider that". In many Eastern European countries business people always wear dark suits and black shoes to a meeting. If you were to wear a grey sports jacket, contrasting dark slacks, and light grey shoes, your choice of dress might be considered a slight against your hosts. In addition, when travelling in Europe, the farther east you go the more frequently people shake hands: always when they first meet each day, and sometimes several times afterward, if they are parted for a time and then rejoin each other.

As world markets expand and boundaries between countries become less apparent, we need to become even more sensitive to the cultural differences that affect how people from other cultures act and react to the way we conduct ourselves and particularly to the way we present information.

If you are going to be doing business with other nations, we suggest you research business communication standards in the country you will be corresponding with or visiting.

Chapter 6

BUSINESS WRITING LANGUAGE

Previous chapters have shown you how to plan and write business communications that convey information quickly and efficiently. The techniques they describe will help you become a well-organized, effective communicator. However, the effect can be harmed if you use weak, wishy-washy words, write unemphatic, convoluted sentences, and construct uncoordinated, rambling paragraphs. This chapter will show you how to avoid some of the common language handling pitfalls that can often inadvertently downgrade the effectiveness and professionalism of your business messages, reports, and proposals.

The Subtle Impact of Good Language

When business manager Dana Courtland receives a well-written report, she does not consciously notice that its words are well chosen, its sentences are properly formed, and its paragraphs read smoothly and interestingly. She also doesn't know that she's retaining the information in that report far better than she does in poorly written reports. The main impression she gains is of a confident, well-thought-out communication that deserves her attention. It's simply easier for her to read and unknown to her, it's also easier for her to understand and retain. Conversely, if she receives a letter in which there are vague or misspelled words, incomplete sentences, or inadequately developed paragraphs, she gains the impression of a person who is careless, unemphatic, and disorganized. She also doesn't know that she's not understanding what's being conveyed and she's not going to remember as much of this information. By inference, Dana may assume the letter contains only routine or unimportant information or she may just ignore it all together.

First, we'll discuss paragraphs and show how you can shape them to achieve a coherent, efficient flow of information. Then we'll look at sentences and examine how they can be sharpened to create a strong impact. Third, we'll show you how to choose and use words effectively. Along the way, we'll also look at some structural implications, including how to punctuate sentences and paragraphs, how to use the Pyramid Method of Writing ™ to direct readers' attention within a paragraph, and how to use abbreviations and numbers in a narrative in a consistent and professional way.

Constructing Coherent Paragraphs

In previous chapters we have used the Pyramid Method of Writing ™ to structure our messages. We can also use a scaled down version of the pyramid to design paragraphs. For a paragraph, the Summary Statement is known as the Topic Sentence. The Topic Sentence is the *main message* that the paragraph is conveying. Then, the supporting details follow, and they're known as the *supporting sentences*, as show in Figure 6-1.

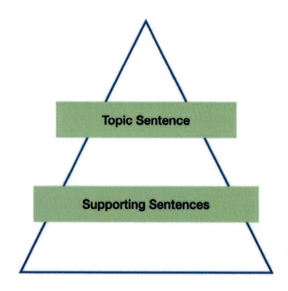

Figure 6-1: The Pyramid writing plan applied to a paragraph

A paragraph structured using the Pyramid Method™ is easy to read:

The meeting achieved only one of its three objectives. The committee approved a $6000 budget increase for the Beta project, but deferred approval of the proposed seven-week extension to the Arbutus program until Mr. Copthorne has submitted a progress report. The committee also decided to delay approving the request for six additional hires until the project group leaders provide detailed job descriptions.

The topic sentences (in italics) is always a general overview that sums up the main points. The remaining sentences then provide the details about that topic. And sometimes, there is a final sentence that draws a *mini conclusion* to that paragraph *or* points the way ahead as in this second paragraph.

Topic Sentence	The Human Resource Department says that 30% of the job applications we receive are rejected because of careless preparation. They cite three main causes
Supporting Sentences	1. failure to answer all of the questions on the form, 2. answers which do not address the questions, and 3. one-sentence answers when a paragraph-form answer is clearly called for.
Mini Conclusion	The HR staff claims that the care an applicant takes in completing the form is an indicator of the applicant's potential as a quality employee.

Develop Good Information Flow

To be effective, a paragraph must carry a reader smoothly from its opening sentences to its closing sentence and must impress a reader with the logic of its development. This means searching for a general narrative pattern, which in most cases is

- chronological order,
- cause to effect, or
- evidence to conclusion.

These patterns are not meant to be so rigid that they inhibit how you write. For example, the 'meetings' paragraph quoted earlier, is in chronological order, and the 'application forms' paragraph progresses generally from cause to effect. The importance of finding a pattern and adhering to it becomes apparent in the following two paragraphs of an incident report.

An incoherent paragraph with poor continuity (chronological sequence)

> The accident occurred when the warehouse maintenance person overrode the brake system on an automated package picker. Another warehouse worker saw the accident and called 911. On Monday, July 20, a package picker slammed to the ground and threw out the maintenance worker who was on it. The worker had found a way to override the brake system on the automated package picker. This reduced his time moving as he performed maintenance procedures on the shelving. He did it using heavy duty packing tape and pushing down the brake. He was taken to the emergency room with minor injuries and will be written up for not following safety protocols.

A coherent paragraph with good continuity (chronological sequence)

> The accident occurred when the warehouse maintenance person overrode the brake system on an automated package picker. He determined that, using heavy duty packing tape, he could push down the brake and move the cart faster. This reduced his time moving as he performed maintenance on the shelving. On Monday, July 20, while in the override mode, the package picker was slammed to the ground, and thrown from the picker. Another warehouse employee saw him and immediately called 911. The maintenance worker was taken to the emergency room with minor injuries and will report back to work on Friday, July 24. He will also be written up for not following proper safety protocols.

Within each paragraph there also needs to be continuity between the sentences, to build bridges as the reader progresses from one thought to the next. This paragraph is choppy because it is composed of a series of separate thoughts. And this choppiness makes it much more difficult to understand.

Choppy Continuity

The supervisors resented being told they had to join the union. They knew they were part of management. They had checked that the same rule did not apply in other companies. They were annoyed their opinion had not been solicited. They asked to meet with the company president.

This choppy, staccato writing is unclear because your audience needs words that connect and bridge the thoughts from one sentence to the next. Without these words, the entire messages loses some of its key meaning. The next paragraph is smoother because it refers to previous expressions and repeats key words ("As supervisors they," "They had also," "And they were," and "So they prepared...").

Smooth Continuity

The supervisors resented being told they had to join the union. As supervisors, they knew that they were traditionally part of management. They had also checked with supervisors at other companies and found the rule did not apply there. And they were annoyed that management had not even asked for their opinion. So they prepared a brief requesting a meeting with the company president.

Parallelism also plays an important role in building paragraph rhythm and continuity, just as it does in building sentence rhythm. In a paragraph that is internally parallel, the verbs (and sometimes adverbs, nouns, and adjectives) have a similar form: a form the reader readily recognizes as rhythm. For example, two expressions are repeated in the paragraph below ("Perhaps...and...," and "Or you..."), which makes readers feel comfortable as they progress through the stages described in the paragraph.

There are various occasions when you will need to present information to a small audience. Perhaps you will attend a seminar or equipment demonstration and, on your return, you will be expected to brief other members of your department. Or you may develop a new process or procedure and have to describe its advantages to other department supervisors. Perhaps visitors will tour your offices and you will be asked to brief them on the work you do. Or you may visit a government department where you have to make a pitch for zoning adjustments. Whatever the circumstances, you will be selling ideas.

These are only brief examples of the many ways you can develop skill in creating continuity within paragraphs you write. To find more information, refer to one of the many resources. One we consider excellent is *The Elements of Style* by William Strunk, Jr. and E. B. White.

Make Subparagraphs Work for You

Subparagraphing is an excellent way to help readers *see* how you are grouping or separating your ideas. Here are some tips to help you write great subparagraphs that help your reader understand the logic of your writing:

- Let the reader see how you are subordinating ideas by indenting the whole subparagraph as a complete block of information, as is being done here. Don't let subsequent lines run back under the paragraph number, bullet, or heading. If you use sub-subparagraphs, indent them as a complete unit too.

- Either number the subparagraphs or use bullets, as is being done here. For numbers versus bullets, follow these rules: Use numbers if you

  - are providing information in a sequence,

  - you want to show the priority of the ideas, or

  - will refer to the subparagraph later in the document.

At all other times, use bullets.

- If a subparagraph contains more than one sentence, write it "pyramid-style": start with a topic sentence and then let subsequent sentences provide amplification (see how this has been done in the two previous bulleted subparagraphs).

- Always insert an introductory sentence to lead into the subparagraphs; We call this a "lead-in line". Don't insert a heading and then immediately start with bullets or numbers.

Punctuate your lead-in line and subsequent subparagraphs like this:

- If the lead-in line is a complete sentence, follow it with a colon, start each subparagraph with a capital letter, and close the subparagraph with a period:

> When ordering supplies, follow these steps:
>
> 1. Click the button, **Placing and Order**.
>
> 2. Click on **Form 2820**.
>
> 3. Type in the order number in the field.
>
> 4. Insert the required quantity and a full description of the item.
>
> 5. Click on the appropriate **Delivery** Instruction entry.
>
> 6. Click **Save** to save the order form.

- If the lead-in line is not a complete sentence, *do not* follow it with a colon; Leave it open. Start each subparagraph with a *lowercase* letter and close the subparagraph with a comma, except the last subparagraph, which must close with a period. Insert the word "and" after the comma at the end of the second-last subparagraph. It's easier to understand when you see the example below.

> When ordering supplies
>
> 1. click the button, **Placing and Order**,
>
> 2. click on **Form 2820**,
>
> 3. type in the order number in the field,
>
> 4. insert the required quantity and a full description of the item,
>
> 5. click on the appropriate **Delivery** Instruction entry, and
>
> 6. click **Save** to save the order form.

- When using the "closed" style of a lead-in line (with a colon at the end), your subparagraphs may contain more than one sentence. However, when using the "open" style of lead-in line (no colon at the end), your subparagraphs cannot contain more than one sentence, because they are really all part of one long sentence shown as a series of steps.

Forming Strong, Confident Sentences

There are two ways you can write the following piece of information:

    A.   The site drawings were erased accidently by Paul Winslett.
    B.   Paul Winslett accidentally erased the site drawings.

As both sentences contain exactly the same information, we can argue for a long time over which is the better way to present these particular facts. Many people prefer sentence A because it is more general and does not try to blame Paul. Practical business people, however, prefer sentence B because they understand the power of its directness.

Use the Active Voice

In business, it is much better to be direct and for the reader, direct writing is much easier to read. So, use a simple subject-verb-object construction that describes "who did what":

Subject (who or what)	Verb (did)	Object (what)
1. The accountant	completed	the audit.
2. Briana	calculated	the project schedule.
3. A power outage	shut down	the production line.
4. The staff	presented	a retirement gift to Abe.

This direct form of writing is known as the **active voice** because it actively conveys information. The example in Sentence 2, above, is written in the active voice. In contrast, sentence A is written in the **passive voice**, because it provides information only passively. We can see its blandness if we convert the four previous sentences into the passive voice style: "what was done by whom".

1.   The audit has been completed by the accountant.
2.   The expenses were calculated by Briana.
3.   The production line was shut down by a power outage.
4.   A retirement gift was presented by the committee to Abe.

Notice the word "by" in each of these passive voice sentences: it can be a signal that you are writing in the passive voice. It shows that something is being done by someone or something. The word "by" does not appear in the four active voice sentences. Also notice some form of the verb "to be". When you see some form of the verb "to be" and it is followed with "by", you are most likely writing in the passive voice. Here are some of the forms of the verb "to be". For a more thorough list of all forms, search the internet.

Subject	Past Tense	Present Tense	Future Tense
I	Was	Am	Will
You	Were	Are	Will
He/She	Was	Is	Will
You (plural)	Were	Are	Will
They	Were	Are	will

Comparing two paragraphs, one constructed mainly of passive voice sentences and one constructed mainly of active voice sentences, clearly demonstrates the difference:

Passive Voice

It was estimated by Jack Herzing that the project will last 15 months. During the initial four months, designs are to be submitted by the architect for approval by Ms. Simpson. A further nine months will be required by the construction company before the new building can be occupied by the mainframe installers. And then, it will take two more months for an internal layout plan and an occupation schedule to be prepared by the phase-in team.

Active Voice

Jack Herzing estimated the project will last 15 months. The architects will submit designs for Ms. Simpson to approve during the first four months. The construction company will require nine months, after which the mainframe installers will begin work. The phase-in team will then require two months to plan the internal layout and prepare an occupation schedule.

The active voice offers two immediate advantages: it is shorter (in the above example, 57 words compared with 77 words for the passive voice), and its verbs are much more emphatic.

Let's review these two paragraphs. In the passive voice examples, we've bolded the forms of the verb "to be" and the word "by" to help you learn how to spot the passive voice quickly and easily. Also, look into the settings of your writing software. Most of them have a setting that will automatically flag the use of passive voice.

Passive Voice	Active Voice
It *was* estimated *by* Jack Herzing...	Jack Herzing estimated...
designs *are to be* submitted *by*...	The architects will submit...
for approval *by* Ms. Simpson...	for Ms. Simpson to approve...
will be required *by* the construction company...	the construction company will require...
can be occupied *by* the equipment installers...	the equipment installers will move in...
to be prepared *by* the phase-in team...	the phase-in team will prepare...

If you can reduce word count by 25%, your readers will love you. Think about it: This is just one short paragraph but what if you are writing a comprehensive proposal that is 50 pages? You can reduce that to 38 pages. Now, which report would you rather read? The active voice action verbs make a writer seem much more confident and, by inference, more competent. We are not implying you have to use the active voice all the time, but we do know that far too many people write in the passive voice too much. To write in the active voice means naming who or what performed the action:

Dana Rooke submitted a five-page proposal for the marketing team.

Head Office transferred Harvey Wahl to the West Haven branch.

Management hired two summer interns to work from May to August.

However, if you do not know or prefer not to name the person or group performing the action, then you have to write in the passive voice. Here's an example:

The shipment of spare parts for Acme Industries has been lost.

However, you could still write this in the active voice. Here's how:

Someone lost the shipment of spare parts destined for Acme Industries.

This may seem to place unnecessary emphasis on an unknow entry: *Someone*. Alternatively try to generalize a "doer" (someone or something) you can name as the subject performing the action:

Rather than write	Try writing
Five cars have been vandalized in the parking lot.	Vandals damaged five cars in the parking lot.
The capital purchases budget has been cut by $86,500.	The controller has cut the capital budget by $86,500.
The space heater was left running all night.	An office employee left the space heater running all night.

Remember, the active voice creates a much stronger, more emphatic impression and is much easier to comprehend and remember than the passive voice. You can test your skills of writing in the active voice by trying Exercise 6-1 at the end of this chapter. The answers are in the back of this book.

Write in the First Person

If you were taught not to start an email, report, proposal, or letter with the pronoun "I," you are probably writing in an unnaturally roundabout way. When writing any correspondence in which you clearly write from one person to another, we recommend that you use the first person ("I"). Using "I" will help you write more easily and more directly. Or, if you feel uncomfortable writing "I" when reporting for your company or organization, then you can write "we" and be just as direct and emphatic. For example:

Using the personal pronouns "I" or "we"	Avoiding the personal pronouns "I" or "we"
I checked the files and found two discrepancies.	The files were checked and two discrepancies were found.

I ordered a site license for the 4TELL software program.	A site license has been ordered for the 4TELL software program.
We have examined our records and can identify only the first of the two invoices you listed in your email.	Our records have been examined and only the first of the two invoices you listed has been identified.

Did you notice that the words "by someone" are implied in each of the sentences in the right column? Did you also notice that each one had some form of the verb "to be"? Take a look:

The files *were* checked (by someone) and...

A site license *has been* ordered (by someone) for...

Our records *have been* examined (by someone) and...

This shows the sentences are written in the passive voice; Although it is hidden, they still contain the identifier "by" and they all contain a form of the verb "to be". When you avoid writing in the first person, you very often slip into the bad habit of writing in the passive voice. So, write in the first person and you are more likely to write in the active voice.

As a general guideline, use "I" when writing email, reports, proposals, or letters in which you present your ideas, thoughts, and opinions or when you describe what you have done. Use "we" when writing email, reports, proposals, or letters that represent your company's views, or when writing on behalf of a group of people or an organization.

Position Words for Maximum Effect

The most powerful element of a communication encounter is the beginning and the ending. The same is true in your writing, as we have seen from The Pyramid Method of Writing ™. The same is true of your sentences. The first and last words in a sentence have potential to create particular emphasis, *provided that you put effective words there*. Too often, however, these high-impact positions are stolen by unimportant words or expressions that reduce the effectiveness of the sentence. For example:

For your information, from June until August, we will condense our workweeks to Monday through Thursday and take Fridays off.

Don't waste the chance to give your sentence power. Remove the redundant expression "For your information," and rearrange the remaining words so that the key words occupy the high-impact positions; the sentence (and people's impression of you) become much stronger.

From June until August, we will condense our workweeks to Monday through Thursday and take Fridays off.

Especially check that conditional words and phrases such as *without a doubt, however, at least, such matters as,* and *without exception to* do not sneak into these positions because they particularly reduce emphasis and steal the power of your sentence.

Instead of	Write
The January meeting has been cancelled, however.	The January meeting, however, has been cancelled.
Without exception, upload troubleshooting reports to the customer support file share by 3 p.m. daily at the latest.	Upload daily troubleshooting reports to the customer support file share no later than 3 p.m.
Be sure to log out of your investment account every hour, at least.	Log out of your investment account once every hour.

Write Structurally Sound Sentences

A structurally unsound sentence can disturb readers, who will be vaguely aware that something is not quite right, even if they do not recognize the reason for it. This, in turn, can deflect their attention from the point you are trying to make. The remedy is to make every sentence work for you by keeping it simple, ensuring it has rhythm, and checking it is complete.

Develop only one thought

A sentence like the one below will force a reader to stumble and go back over the words to find out what its writer is trying to say:

There has been a documentation problem in calculating the project costs, which Ms. Smythe brought to the committee's attention on May 18, but at now it is considered unimportant, because Mr. Cordon claimed it would

not seriously affect the schedule, and will result in a three-day delay before we can meet with the client to discuss progress payments.

Readers will have trouble because its writer has forgotten the most important rule of writing a sentence: **Develop only one thought in each sentence.**

Although a sentence can have several subordinate clauses, they all must evolve from or support a single thought or idea. To make the above sentence coherent and understandable to the reader, the writer must divide it into at least two sentences, each developing a separate thought:

Sentence 1:

There has been a documentation problem in calculating project costs, which will result in a three-day delay before we can meet with the client to discuss progress payments.

Central thought: There will be a delay.

Sentence 2:

Ms. Smythe predicted this at the May 18 meeting, but it was considered unimportant because Mr. Cordon claimed it would not seriously affect the schedule.

Central thought: The problem was predicted but ignored.

The original sentence also violated a useful guideline concerning sentence length: we suggest that, on average, a sentence should not exceed 25-30 words. The original, long sentence contained 63 words; the two revised sentences each contain less than 30 words.) However, this guideline is just that, only a guideline. The sentence length can be affected by the complexity of the topic and your knowledge of the reader. Here are two more ideas that augment this:

- If a sentence is describing a very general topic for a knowledgeable reader, it can be as long as the rewritten sentences above, or even a little longer.

- If the topic is complex, or if you suspect the reader may have difficulty understanding it, then on average, the sentences should be no longer than 15-20 words.

Write complete sentences

Every day we see examples of incomplete sentences, and this is getting much worse as people use text messaging to type snippets of information. We may also see these in advertising text where the writers use them to create a crisp, intentionally choppy effect, which may serve their purpose well for the audiences they are trying to reach. Here's an example of short, choppy advertising copy for an airline:

Sheer Comfort!

37,000 feet high. Wide Seats, just like in your living room. Tempting meals when you ask for them. Complimentary refreshments. Only on Remick Airlines. Our Business Class. Try it!

If we do the same in our business or technical writing, our readers will not be happy. Nor will they be able to understand what we are trying to convey. A common and very easy error to make, particularly when your writing is going well and you do not want to interrupt your enthusiasm, is to inadvertently form a sentence fragment. For example:

- The meeting achieved its objective. Even though three members were absent.

- The operators were encouraged to leave at 3 p.m. Being the hottest day of the year.

In most cases a sentence fragment can be corrected by removing the period that separates it from the sentence it depends on, inserting a comma in place of the period, and adding a conjunction or connecting word such as *and, but, which, who,* or *because:*

- The meeting achieved its objective, even though three members were absent. ↑

- The operators were encouraged to leave at 3 p.m., *because it was* the hottest day of the year. ↑ ↑

Note: We replaced *being* with *because it was.*

Here are two more:

- Staff will have to eat at their desks or go out for lunch from October 6 to 10. While we renovate the lunchroom.

Change the period to a comma.

Staff will have to eat at their desks or go out for lunch from October 6 to 10, while we renovate the lunchroom. ↑

- All 20-year employees will receive a length-of-service award. Including three who retired earlier this year.

Change the period to a comma.

- All 20-year employees will receive a length-of-service award, including three who retired earlier this year. ↑

In particular, check sentences that start with a word that ends in "—ing". Here are some to watch out for: *referring, answering, being.* Also check expressions that end in "...to", like this: *with reference to.*

- With reference to your letter of June 6. We have considered your request and will be sending you a check.

Change the period to a comma.

- With reference to your letter of June 6, we have considered your request and will be sending you a check. ↑

Alternately, you could restructure the sentence, and this is the stronger, more effective structure.

- We have considered the request in your letter of June 6 and will be sending you a check.
- Referring to the problem of vandalism to employee's automobiles in the parking lot. We will be hiring a security guard to patrol the area from 8 a.m. to 6 p.m., Monday through Friday.

Although the period could be changed to a comma, we recommend restructuring the fragment to form a better sentence.

- To resolve the problem of vandalism to employee's automobiles in the parking lot, we will be hiring a security guard to patrol the area from 8 a.m. to 6 p.m., Monday through Friday.

A similar sentence error occurs if you link two separate thoughts in a single sentence, joining them with only a comma or even no punctuation. The effect can jar a reader uncomfortably.

- Marie Shields has been selected for the engineering conference on May 8, she is very excited to attend.

This awkward construction is known as a **run-on** sentence and it is grammatically incorrect. It's also confusing to a reader. It can be corrected in two ways:

- Replace the comma with a period to form two complete sentences:

Marie Shields has been selected for the engineering conference on May 8. She is very excited to attend.

- Retain the comma and follow it with *and, which* or *but*:

Marie Shields has been selected for the engineering conference on May 8, *and* she is very excited to attend.

Marie Shields has been selected for the engineering conference on May 8, *which* she is very excited to attend.

A run-on sentence with *no* punctuation is even more noticeable:

- The customer claims he has not received an invoice I made up a new one.

We see more and more of this now in the age of texting, and it's very confusing in business writing. And that confusion can lead to some very big mistakes. So, here's how to easily correct it. Put either a period or a comma followed by a linking word between *invoice* and *I*:

- The customer claims he has not received an invoice. I made up a new one.

- The customer claims he has not received an invoice, so, I made up a new one.

It's surprising how easily such simple sentence or punctuation faults can slip by unnoticed—until they reach your reader—who immediately notices them! To test your punctuation skills, try Exercise 6-2 at the end of this chapter.

Keep the Parts Parallel

Just as listeners may not consciously notice rhythm until a musician strikes a discordant note, readers often do not notice sentence parallelism until they stumble over a non-parallel sentence. For example,

> The supervisor predicted the problem and was quick in recommending corrective action.

We understand what this writer is saying, but the sentence lacks rhythm because its two verbs (predicated and recommending) are not in the same form. The expression *quick in recommending* needs to be changed so that it is parallel with *predicted*. The result is a much stronger, more defined statement that your reader can read and retain much easier.

> The supervisor *predicted* the problem and quickly *recommended* corrective action.

Parallelism becomes especially important when joining two parts of a sentence with a coordinating conjunction such as

- *and* (as in the above example),

- *or*,

- *but*,

- a comma, or

- a correlative such as *either...or; neither...nor;* or *not only...but also*.

Here are three examples:

Change	When the Calgary branch closed, we *transferred* four staff members to other branches and *arrangements were made* for two to retire early.
To	When the Calgary branch closed, we *transferred* four staff members to other branches and *arranged* for two to retire.
Change	You can either *take* the remainder of your vacation time in December or it *can be deferred* until next year.
To	You can either *take* the remainder of your vacation time in December or *defer* it until next year.

Notice the writer wrote the first two in the passive voice. We used the active voice to make them parallel. Parallelism is also important when compiling a list of steps. For example,

When the project is complete, write a project completion report and distribute it as follows:

1. Attach two copies to the contract and email them to the client.

2. Send one copy to the accountant, with a request that the final invoice be sent to the client.

3. File two copies in the appropriate place on our file server.

4. The final step is to write an email to each of the branch managers informing them the report is complete and attach your report to it. The email should state that the report is for information only, and that they don't have to do anything.

In steps 2 and 4, the verbs are not parallel with those in steps 1 and 3. In step 2, the second part of the sentence ("with a request that they send the final invoice to the client") is not parallel with the first half of the sentence. To make this much easier on your reader, revise step 2 like this (see italicized words):

2. *Send* one copy to the accountant. *Include* a statement authorizing the accountant to send the final invoice to the client.

In step 4, the structure of the whole paragraph is not parallel with the previous steps. Revise it like this:

4. *Write* an email to each of the branch managers. *State* that the project is *complete*, the report is *attached* and is for information only, and that no action is required. *Attach* the report to the email.

Choosing the Right Words

The right word used at the right moment and in the right place can create exactly the right effect. Unfortunately, we have allowed ourselves to become a generation of lazy word-users: we often use vague, undescriptive, readily available, or cliché words instead of taking the time to find words that do a much better, more effective job to convey exactly what we mean.

I was held up because I helped some people whose vehicle went into the ditch.

The vagueness of this sentence plants numerous questions in the reader's minds.

How long were you held up?
What did you do to help?
What vehicle?
How did it get into the ditch?
Where did this happen?
Was anyone injured?

Remember, effective communication means we answer the anticipated questions of our readers. So, use words that paint pictures in your reader's mind.

Use Words that Paint Pictures

Just by changing a few words, you can be much more explicit and answer the reader's questions:

I was delayed 40 minutes while I helped pull two passengers from a Honda Odyssey that had rolled into the ditch 2 km north of Tate's Corner. Neither were injured.

Look at these simple changes that make this so much more effective:

held up	has become	delayed 40 minutes
helped	has become	helped pull
some people	has become	two passengers
vehicle	has become	Honda Odyssey
went	has become	rolled
a ditch	has become	a ditch 2 km north of Tate's Corner

The tendency to grab any vague, easy-to-find word rather than to think of a more descriptive word not only can obscure a message but also may delay or confuse communication. Vague communication can lead to wasted time because your reader has to ask questions. That can lead to a lot of back and forth that you could have avoided by using more focused, precise language. As technical communicators it is our responsibility to anticipate what our readers want to know, and then use clear, descriptive words to provide the facts in a way they can best understand the message.

Here's some important tips:

When you are tempted to write...	Pause first and then think of more precise words such as...
contacted, communicated with	emailed, texted, talked to, video conferenced
put, placed	threw, slid into, rammed, handed, placed, dropped, positioned, inserted
got, picked up	bought, were given, borrowed, rented, purchased
went, sent	drove, flew, cycled, walked, emailed, texted, shipped

See the difference! Read these following sentences and see how more explicit words improve clarity:

- We *went* to Edmonton.   Change to   We *flew* to Edmonton.
- We are *getting* new CAD software.   Change to   We *ordered* new CAD software.
- I *sent* the report May 1.   Change to   I *emailed* the report May 1.
- I put away the telescope.   Change to   I stored the telescope in room 106A and locked it.

Use Specifics Rather than Generalizations

Compare these two month-end progress reports and decide whether Jane or Janet has written the better report:

Jane: The Arbutus program is moving along nicely and should be completed easily by the end of the month.

Janet: The Nova project is 70% complete. Although currently three days behind schedule, it will still be finished by November 30, as planned.

We have found that usually, opinion is divided, with half of our readers choosing Jane's report and half preferring Janet's. However, what happens if we rephrase the question, like this: Compare these two month-end progress reports and decide which of these two report writers you think has the better handle on the job?

This time, over 80% of readers will answer: "Janet!" Why? Because her use of *specifics* persuades them she has everything under control.

Jane's report makes her seem pleasantly but only hazily competent, whereas Janet's makes her sound sure of herself because *she has quoted exact quantities and dates.* Readers are more inclined to believe and have confidence in writers who use strong, definite words and quote exact, rather than vague, information.

Select Short Rather than Long Words

When searching for descriptive words you have to take care that you do not go to the other extreme and start using large, lesser-used words that can often sound ponderous and pompous rather than clear and specific. An accountant who describes an employee's salary as "remuneration" and the company pension plan as the "superannuation scheme" has allowed this to happen. So has a computer programmer who refers to "sophisticated diagnostic techniques" when she really means complex troubleshooting methods. A manager who describes how her staff has "furthered their competence" could be much more effective by just saying that her staff has gained new skills.

The problem with such overblown words is that they *look* impressive. When you see them in print, you hesitate to tamper with them, as if they were carved in stone. There are three solid reasons for not using overblown words:

1. Your reader may not understand what you have written. Think of someone whose second language may be your first. They can comprehend simpler words so you can more effectively convey your message. Think about your skills using a second language. If you were reading in that second language, wouldn't you want the writer to use shorter words?

2. You may not fully understand their exact meaning, so you use them incorrectly (and your reader could easily know this). For instance, how many of you thought the word "remuneration" used above should have been "renumeration"? If you did, you would have been wrong. Even though a lot of people use it, "renumeration" is not a word.

3. You may seem pompous or overbearing (or both) to your reader. Often, people equate using big words with trying to impress. Don't impress. Communicate effectively.

Sometimes you will have to use big words, such as "reverberation," because there is no simpler word you can use as a substitute. At all other times, you should choose a simple but exact word that both you *and* your reader will recognize and understand. Remember the cautionary remarks made by an economy-minded business executive:

Never us a 75-cent word when a perfectly sound 30-cent word exists which you can use just as successfully.

Eliminate Wordy Expressions (LICs)

We have become so accustomed to seeing other writers use wordy expressions that we tend to think it's all right for us to use them too. Not so. Professional technical communicators know that these expressions just confuse and make more work for the reader. A wordy expression is any word or group of words that, when either removed from or shortened within a sentence, does not change the meaning of the sentence. For example, at first glance these sentences seem properly constructed:

1. A new office is being built in close proximity to London, Ontario.
2. The committee was in agreement with Mr. Hanson's proposal.
3. Ms. Reynaud estimated that the new procedure would result in a $50,000 increase in operating costs annually.
4. It is our considered opinion that you should make a concerted effort to reduce overhead costs.

Yet each of these sentences would sound more emphatic if we eliminated or shortened them.

1. A new office is being built close to London, Ontario.
    (*in...proximity* has been deleted)

2. The committee agreed with Mr. Hanson's proposal.
    (*was in agreement with* has been shortened to *agreed*)

3. Ms. Reynaud estimated that the new procedure would decrease operating costs by $50,000 annually.
    (*result in* has been deleted)

4. We believe you should reduce your overhead costs.
   (*It is our considered opinion* has been shortened to *We believe,* and *make a concerted effort to* has been deleted)

The words we have deleted are known as low-information content (LIC) expressions. When you remove them from a sentence, the sentence contains no less information; in fact; often the sentence is improved. Compare these two examples of the same piece of information:

Wordy Original:

> It is a matter of concern that it has been brought to my attention that in the course of the past three months no track has been kept of how many kilograms of metal have been purchased for engineering students' prototypes. At this point in time you are hereby advised that it will be necessary to keep a running record, involving entry into a log sheet that is kept on a common server. Be sure that you remember to log every kilogram ordered.

With the wordy expression removed, and the remaining words rearranged slightly, the message *immediately* becomes clear:

Simpler Version:

> I am concerned that for three months, you have not been tracking metal used for our engineering student's prototypes. From now on, please log all orders and the exact kilograms ordered into the log sheet file named ENG_ORDER_Metal.exe.

Table 6-2 contains a list of common wordy expressions. Expressions you should avoid completely are marked with an X. Alternatives are given for expressions that need to be shortened. Table 6-3 contains a list of clichés or overused expressions that also contribute to wordiness. You should avoid using all of the phrases in Table 6-2. You can practice removing LICs in Exercise 6-4 at the end of the chapter.

Expression	Avoid	Shorten to
actually	X	
as necessary	X	
at present	X	
at this time	X	
in color (colour)	X	
in length	X	

in number	X	
in size	X	
in fact; in point of fact	X	
in light of	X	
is a person who	X	
on the part of	X	
a number of		many; several
as a means of		for; to
as a result		so
at the rate of		at
at the same time as		while
bring to a conclusion		conclude
by means of; by use of		by
communicate with		talk to; email; write
connected together		connected
due to the fact that		because
during the course of		during
during the time that		while
end result		result
exhibits a tendency to		tends to
for a period of		for
for the purpose of		for; to
for the reason that		because
for this reason		because
in all probability		probably
in an area where		where
in an effort to		to
in close proximity to		close to; near
in connection with		about
in order to		to
in such a manner as to		to
in terms of		in; for
in the course of		during
in the direction of		toward
in the event that		If
in the form of		as
in the vicinity of		about; near; approximately
involves the necessity of		demands; requires
is designed to be		is
it can bee seen that		thus; so
it is considered desirable to		I/we want to
it will be necessary to		I/we must
of considerable magnitude		large

on account of	because
previous to; prior to	before
subsequent to	after
the majority of	most
with the aid of	with
with the result that	so; therefore

Table 6-2: Typical Low Information Content (LIC) Expressions

a matter of concern	in the foreseeable future
all things being equal	in the long run
and/or	in the matter of
as a last resort	it stands to reason
as a matter of fact	last but not least
as per	needless to say
at this point in time	on the right track
attached hereto	par for the course
conspicuous by its absence	please feel free to
easier said than done	regarding the matter of
enclosed herewith	the stage is set
for your information	this will acknowledge
if and when	we are pleased to advise
in reference to	we wish to state
in short supply	you are hereby advised

Table 6-3: Typical Overused Expressions

Avoid Words that Antagonize

Certain words or combinations of words can have an adverse effect on readers. If you use them you may never realize you have created a negative reaction. For example, if Peter writes to Chris; "I am sure you will agree that," Chris's emotional reaction probably will be *not* to agree! Consequently, you need to tread very carefully before you use any expression that may prove to be mildly antagonistic. Remember, we are writing for results, not writing to express our emotions. Even if you don't mean it, when we write, we are not there in person to express ourselves, so our written words are much more open to our audiences' interpretations. Antagonistic expressions generally fall into three groups:

1. Words that make a reader feel guilty
2. Words that "talk down" to a reader
3. Words which challenge or provoke a reader

Words that make a reader feel guilty

Each of these expressions (and others) can make readers feel you are accusing them of being inadequate or incompetent.

You have overlooked the details outlined in section 14.
You have neglected to sign the buyer's agreement.
You have failed to fill in the previous employment details.
You ought to know that refunds cannot be accepted after 30 days.
You have not understood the specifications.

Words that "talk down" to a reader

These expressions (and others) can make a reader feel as if you think you are superior to him or her.

You must understand our position.
We have to assume from your email that you will not be requesting an interview.
I must request that you attend a meeting in room B101 on February 15.
Undoubtedly you will be purchasing a new unit from us.
We simply do not understand how you reached this decision.

Words which challenge or provoke a reader

These expressions can put your reader on the defense.

Your demand for a refund has been denied.
You must return the paperwork by May 28.
You have erred in completing the test.
We must insist that you comply with the HAZMAT team's safety protocols.
We are sure you will agree that the return-to-work legislation is justified.

Select the Right Word—And Spell It Correctly!

Some words are so similar, it's easy to confuse them. This can lead to miscommunication. And remember, in the professional world, *many people know the difference*. So if you don't, you may be judged as sloppy or ignorant.

Here are some examples:

affect and effect

there; their; and they're

defective and deficient

disinterested and uninterested

Each has a different meaning; so the correct word must be used in the proper content. If you are unsure about a word, its usage or spelling, consult a dictionary. That only takes a moment of your time and it will help you communicate the correct information.

If you really want to use words correctly and have a robust vocabulary to help you express your thoughts and ideas better, we highly recommend you read professional publications, books, and articles. Read a lot and on a regular basis. There is no better way to increase your vocabulary.

How closely do *you* need to depend on a dictionary? If you are not sure, test yourself by completing Exercise 6-5 at the end of this chapter.

Forming Abbreviations

When a long word, such as counterclockwise, or a multiword expression such as document design center, is used repeatedly in a letter or report, it's convenient to abbreviate it to a shorter form. You can abbreviate a word or expression in any way you wish, providing you first tell your readers what the abbreviation means. The first time you use the word, spell it out in full and then show the abbreviated form in brackets immediately after it:

The document design office (ddo) will monitor the new computer reports. If the ddo makes an update, it will inform the company via email.

The following guidelines apply to forming abbreviations:
• Never form a new abbreviation for a word or expression that already has a recognized abbreviation. For example, readers probably would not recognize the abbreviation apx, if you were to use it instead of approx as the abbreviation for approximately. In other words, don't make up your own abbreviations for those that have standards adopted by governing agencies.

- Use lower case letters, unless the abbreviation is formed from a recognized title such as Royal Bank (RB), or is derived from a person's or an organization's name. For example, write kilogram as kg, but kilohertz as kHz (because the first letter of Hz represents a person's name: Hertz).

- Omit internal periods from an abbreviation unless the abbreviation forms another word. For example: write RRC for Red River College and CBC for Canadian Broadcasting Corporation, but in. for inch and a.m. for morning. If the abbreviation happens to be the last word in a sentence, then the abbreviation will end with a period.

- Do not add an "s" after plural abbreviations of quantities; treat them in exactly the same way you would for a singular abbreviation, as in 34 km and 17.4 kg.

Inevitably, there are exceptions to these rules. Traditionally, No. (the abbreviation for *number*) has a capital N. Similarly, in the computer field, RAM is always written in capital letters.

Writing Metric Symbols

The rules for writing, typing, and printing SI (metric) units are rigid but straightforward, with many of them paralleling the guidelines for writing non-metric expressions:

- Type all metric units in upright type, even if they are in a sentence that is set in italic type.

- Use lower case letters for all symbols, except where the letter used in a symbol is formed from a person's name: g for gram, but V for volt (derived from Alessandro Volta).

- Always leave a space between the last numeral of a quantity and the first letter of the symbol: 20 kg, 120 V.

- Do not add an "s" after a plural symbol: 23 kL.

- Do not place a period after the symbol, unless it ends a sentence (see kL immediately above).

- Use an oblique stoke or "forward slash" (/) to represent per, and a dot at midletter height (•) to denote that the symbols on either side of the dot are multiplied.

Writing Numbers Correctly

When you write numbers in a table or as part of a column, you align them at the decimal place, one above the other. When you write them individually as part of a sentence, the rules change slightly. The basic rule is straightforward:

- Spell out numbers from one to nine.

- Use numerals for 10 and above.

However, there are several exceptions you need to know. Always use numerals for

- dimensions, speeds, tolerances, radio frequencies, etc: 5 km/hr,

- any number that is followed by a unit of measure: 3 mm,

- any number that contains a decimal or a fraction: 44.6, 2.5, 2½, and

- percentages, sums of money, book or document chapters and page references, and people's ages.

Always spell out

- any number that starts a sentence (or, better still, restructure the sentence so the number is not at the beginning), and

- any fraction in which the whole number is less than one: two-thirds.

Here are three additional guidelines:

- Always insert a zero before a decimal that is less than one: 0.67.

- Spell out one of the numbers when two consecutive numbers are not separated by punctuation: Thirty 80-kg cartons.

- When a series of large and small numbers appear in a sentence or paragraph, use numerals for all of them: In room 207 there are 4 tables and 16 chairs.

Exercises, Chapter 6

Exercise 6-1: Changing passive voice to active voice

Improve the effectiveness of these sentences by changing them from the passive voice to the active voice.

1. The meeting was adjourned by the chairperson at 4:30 p.m.

2. At Viking Insurance, the call-in question service has been replaced by an online chat service.

3. At its October meeting, it was agreed by the executive of the company's social club that the holiday party should be held on December 6.

4. The product analysis report written by Mavis Barns was edited by Vic Darwin and Illustrated by Rachel Grant.

5. When the Vancourt Business Systems was audited by Revenue Canada, a $30,000 discrepancy was found between reported and actual income.

6. It is recommended that the Jensen Hygiene Protocol be adopted by the company.

7. Work was stopped at 1:55 p.m. by a power outage which lasted 4 hours. At 2:30 p.m. it was decided by the office manager that all employees should go home for the remainder of the day.

8. It was decided by the staff development committee that the request from Terry Rozak for attendance at the April Western Region Business Society meeting should be approved.

9. Although a 17% production loss had been predicted by the manufacturing team for the month of August, the actual production loss reported by Production Control was only 6%.

10. It is of some concern to me that a similar budgeting problem to the one identified by our R&D department has been faced by your company's R&D department.

Turn to page 140 for suggested answers.

Exercise 6-2: Run-on sentence and sentence fragments

Correct any incorrect punctuation you can find in these sentences, particularly punctuation causing run-on sentences and sentence fragments.

1. The red warning label on the bottle read: "Do not give to children weighing less than 30 kg." Definitely not intended for 6-year-olds.

2. I have examined your Nabuchi Model 400 smartphone, repairs will cost you $150 plus tax.

3. We installed 20 new systems, right now we only need 15. Five for a planned expansion next year.

4. I am requesting that you transfer my account from your branch at 1620 Portage Avenue to your new branch at 310 St. Mary's Road, this confirms my email instructions of May 31.

5. With reference to your email confirming the purchase of a new service truck. I have originated a purchase order detailing the price and delivery date. To confirm the order.

6. Please book me flights to Toronto on October 14, return on October 20. Aisle seat preferred.

7. Effective June 1, Shirley Watzinger is to be transferred to the Melbourne office, this confirms my email instructions sent September 4. Salary and benefits to remain the same.

8. In yesterday's email you described a problem with your package shipped to you last week. Purchase order 2720 Invoice 1514A. Received wet and unusable, I have arranged for ZipEx Courier to pick it up. Replace with repeat order, ship within five days.

9. We finished work on the data conversion project March 12. One week ahead of the scheduled completion date, a reason to celebrate!

10. The order from Nesbitt Industries came in by courier at noon on May 27, they had been trying to call us for three days, they had the wrong number.

Turn to page 141 for suggested answers.

Exercise 6-3: Correcting faulty parallelism

Improve the parallelism in the following sentences and short passages.

1. If we buy only three units, the cost will be $187 each, but it will drop to $164 apiece if we buy eight or more units.

2. We selected the model AS800 processor because of its small size, high speed and because it can be used in most of our computers.

3. A questionnaire was distributed to customers in the Southwood Mall not only to assess the public's reaction but also because it was considered a good method for drawing attention to the new product.

4. The main conclusions drawn from the company's job-sharing experiment show that job sharing

- requires compatible participants,

- employee attendance is improved, and

- increases individual productivity.

5. When we tested a new game, DarkBattleIV, before a test group, 64% of the gamers who tested it liked it, but of the potential game sponsors who were also invited to test it, only 18% were complimentary.

6. All shop floor supervisors are to attend an eight-hour health and safety course during which they will be given training in administering first aid and how to recognize and helping heart attack victims.

7. Each new employee will have a medical examination in the morning, and in the afternoon will attend a three-hour company orientation seminar.

8. Jeff Freiberg is to coordinate the project, manager responsibilities have been assigned to Candace Swystun, and a study of the documentation process has been initiated by Hal Kominsky.

9. We have purchased three dozen headsets: 25 model 70A+s for each help desk employee at $39.50; 4 model 70A+s to be held as spare units; and, for the supervisors, 2 model 70As at $29.95 each.

10. The recent downsizing has meant reducing staff by 17 employees, of whom 3 elected early retirement, 4 chose to be transferred to the Brighton office, retraining was chosen by 8 employees and job-sharing was selected by Julie Yousof and Ken Doucette.

Turn to page 142 for suggested answers.

Exercise 6-4: Removing low-information-content (LIC) expressions

Delete or shorten the low-information-content expressions in the following sentences. In some sentences you may have to rearrange the words.

1. Should you experience further trouble in connecting with your account, please feel free to call me at any time.

2. It has come to my attention that the Ardmore Account contains an error of considerable magnitude.

3. For your information, we have transferred your account to the Memphis office.

4. The report brings the Merton project to a successful conclusion.

5. Subsequent to a check of our records, it has been found that you have actually been billed twice.

6. With reference to our analysis of the data, it can be seen that the end result was in the order of 3.6% decrease in market share for the fourth quarter.

7. The employees at the Willowdale office exhibit a tendency to work more overtime than the employees who are located at the Montreal office.

8. There is no advantage at this point in time in trying to identify who was responsible for the error.

9. I am in the process of submitting only an approximate cost estimate due to the fact that there are too many variables to permit me to calculate an exact price.

10. In order to complete the changeover by January 31, it was considered necessary by the executive committee to employ three temporary data input operators for a period of three weeks.

Turn to page 143 for suggested answers.

Exercise 6-5: Selecting the correct words

In each sentence below, identify which is the correctly spelled word or the correct word for the given circumstance. Do this exercise *without* referring to a dictionary.

1. After a (lengthy / lengthly) discussion, the committee agreed to (develope / develop) a new marketing strategy.

2. A (separate / seperate) invoice is to be prepared for each shipment to the Ottawa office.

3. The (amount / number) of houses sold this year was 37 (fewer / less) than the quantity sold last year.

4. By (lightening / lightning) the workload, I hope to achieve better employee (morale / morals).

5. (Similarly / Similarily), the employee must scan each product and match it with the (relevant / revelant) purchase order.

6. Although the supervisor had been (discreet / discrete), the staff (implied / inferred) from her enquiries that there still was a problem.

7. My car was (stationary / stationery) when a truck skidded into it.

8. Although Jamel was keen to hear the labour board's decision, he really was only (a disinterested / an uninterested) observer, because he would not be (affected / effected) by the result.

9. When the Manger of Human Resources tried to (council / counsel) the employee, she also asked questions designed to (elicit / illicit) information from them.

10. The United States needs a better business (environment / enviornment) to encourage its (entrepreneurs / entrepeneurs / entepreneurs).

Turn to page 144 for suggested answers.

Answers to Exercises

Exercise 6-1 Answers

1. The chairperson adjourned the meeting at 4:30 p.m.

2. At Viking Insurance, an online chat service replaced the call-in question service.

3. At its October meeting, the executive of the company's social club agreed to hold the holiday party on December 6.

4. Mavis Barns wrote the product analysis report, Vic Darwin edited it and Rachel Grant illustrated it.

5. When Revenue Canada audited Vancourt Business Systems they found a $30,000 discrepancy between reported and actual income.

6. We recommend the company adopt the Jensen Hygiene Protocol.

7. A 4-hour power outage stopped work at 1:55 p.m. At 2:30 p.m. the office manager decided that all employees should go home for the remainder of the day.

8. The staff development committee decided to approve Terry Rozak's request to attend the April Western Region Business Society meeting.

9. Although the manufacturing team predicted a 17% production loss for August, Production Control reported the actual loss was only 6%.

10. I am concerned that your company has faced a similar budgeting problem to the one our R&D department identified.

Exercise 6-2 Answers

1. The red warning label on the bottle read: "Do not give to children weighing less than 30 kg." The medication was definitely not intended for 6-year-olds.

2. I have examined your Nabuchi Model 400 smartphone. Repairs will cost you $150 plus tax.

3. We installed 20 new systems, although right now we only need 15. Five systems are for a planned expansion next year.

4. I am requesting that you transfer my account from your branch at 1620 Portage Avenue to your new branch at 310 St. Mary's Road. This confirms my email instructions of May 31.

5. I have originated a purchase order detailing the price and delivery date of the new service truck as confirmed in your email.

6. Please book a flight to Toronto for me on October 14, with a return flight on October 20. I prefer an aisle seat.

7. Effective June 1, Shirley Watzinger is to be transferred to the Melbourne office. This confirms my email instructions sent September 4. Her salary and benefits will remain the same.

8. In yesterday's email you described a problem with your package shipped to you last week against Purchase Order 2720 and Invoice 1514A. The package was received wet and unusable so I have arranged for a ZipEx Courier to pick it up. We will replace the order and ship it within five days.

9. We finished work on the data conversion project on March 12, one week ahead of the scheduled completion date: we had a reason to celebrate!

10. The order from Nesbitt Industries came in by courier at noon on May 27. They had been trying to call us for three days, but they had the wrong number.

Exercise 6-3 Answers

1. If we buy only three units, the cost will be $187 each, but if we buy eight or more units it will drop to $164 each.

2. We selected the model AS800 processor because of its small size, high speed and compatibility with most of our computers.

3. A questionnaire was distributed to customers in the Southwood Mall not only to assess the public's reaction but also to draw attention to the new product.

4. The main conclusions drawn from the company's job-sharing experiment show that job sharing

   - requires compatible participants,

   - improves employee attendance, and

   - increases individual productivity.

5. When we tested a new game, DarkBattleIV, before a test group, 64% of the gamers who tested it liked it, but only 18% of the invited potential game sponsors were complimentary.

6. All shop floor supervisors are to attend an eight-hour health and safety course during which they will be given training in administering first aid and recognizing and helping heart attack victims.

7. Each new employee will have a medical examination in the morning, and will attend a three-hour company orientation seminar in the afternoon.

8. Jeff Freiberg is to coordinate the project, Candace Swystun is to assume manager responsibilities and Hal Kominsky is to initiate a study of the documentation process.

9. We have purchased three dozen headsets: 25 model 70A+s for each help desk employee at $39.50, 4 model 70A+s to be held as spare units, and 2 model 70As for the supervisors, at $29.95 each.

10. The recent downsizing has meant reducing staff by 17 employees, of whom 3 elected early retirement, 4 chose to be transferred to the Brighton office, 8 chose retraining and 2 (Julie Yousof and Ken Doucette) selected job-sharing.

Exercise 6-4 Answers

1. If you experience further trouble with your account, please call me.

2. I noticed that the Ardmore Account contains a large error.

3. We have transferred your account to the Memphis office.

4. The report concludes the Merton project.

5. Our records show that you have been billed twice.

6. Our analysis of the data, shows a 3.6% decrease in market share for the fourth quarter.

7. The employees at the Willowdale office tend to work more overtime than the employees at the Montreal office.

8. There is no advantage in trying to identify who was responsible for the error.

9. I am in the process of submitting a cost estimate because we found there are too many variables to calculate an exact price.

10. To complete the changeover by January 31, the executive committee decided to employ three temporary data input operators for three weeks.

Exercise 6-5 Answers

1. After a (**lengthy** / ~~lengthly~~) discussion, the committee agreed to (~~develope~~ / **develop**) a new marketing strategy.

2. A (**separate** / ~~seperate~~) invoice is to be prepared for each shipment to the Ottawa office.

3. The (~~amount~~ / **number**) of houses sold this year was 37 (**fewer** / ~~less~~) than the quantity sold last year.
    Use amount *and* less *when referring to quantities you cannot count, and* number *and* fewer *for quantities you can count.*

4. By (**lightening** / ~~lightning~~) the workload, I hope to achieve better employee (**morale** / ~~morals~~).
    Lightening *means to make lighter.* Lightning *refers to an atmospheric discharge of electricity.* Moral *refers to personal strength of character and the ability to differentiate between right and wrong.* Morale *refers to the general contentedness and state of motivation of a person or group of people.*

5. (**Similarly** / ~~Similarily~~), the employee must scan each product and match it with the (**relevant** / ~~revelant~~) purchase order.

6. Although the supervisor had been (**discreet** / ~~discrete~~), the staff (~~implied~~ / **inferred**) from her enquiries that there still was a problem.
    Discreet *means to have discretion.* Discrete *refers to two separate entities. A person who speaks or writes can* imply; *a person who listens to or reads something can* infer *from what they have heard or read.*

7. My car was (**stationary** / ~~stationery~~) when a truck skidded into it.
    Stationary *refers to something that is not moving.* Stationery *refers to paper products like writing paper.*

8. Although Jamel was keen to hear the labour board's decision, he really was only (**a disinterested** / ~~an uninterested~~) observer, because he would not be (**affected** / ~~effected~~) by the result.
    Disinterested *means to be uninvolved, unbiased or impartial.* Uninterested *means to be not interested.* Affect *is a verb.* Effect *is a noun..*

9. When the Manger of Human Resources tried to (~~council~~ / **counsel**) the employee, she also asked questions designed to (**elicit** / ~~illicit~~) information from them.

A Council *is a body of people.* To counsel *means to give advice.* Elicit *means to find out.* Illicit *means illegal.*

10. The United States needs a better business (**environment** / ~~enviornment~~) to encourage its (**entrepreneurs** / ~~entrepeneurs~~ / ~~entepreneurs~~).

Centre for Technical and Engineering Leadership

When engineers, technologists and technicians are promoted from within, they have the technical knowledge to excel, but do they have the leadership skills they need to be successful?

Courses Specifically Designed for Engineers

Managing Projects	Managing Conflict
Listening Skills	Oral Presentations
Managing Time	Ethics and Technology
Understanding Personality Types	Letter and Report Writing
Meeting Skills	Data Privacy and Security
Intercultural Communication	Discovering Your own Innovation
Elements of Critical Thinking	Leadership Models and Icons

42 years of experience putting the P in the P. Eng.

CTEL offers open registration and in-house programs. Call for details 866-744-3032 or see www.rgilearning.com

 a subsidiary